Simple Solutions For Selling

A Simple Approach to Train Your Sales & Management Team

By Milo Mannino

www.SolutionsForSelling.com

2012 Simple Solutions For Selling

Mannino, Milo
    Simple Solutions For Selling: A Simple Approach to Train Your Sales & Management Team

ISBN-10: 0615672701
ISBN-13: 978-0615672700

Printed in the United States of America.

Table of Contents

Acknowledgements

The creation of this book has been an amazing journey. Through the many years of my life travels, I've learned many lessons. Making time for my family is one of the biggest for me. The love I have for them is immeasurable and I cherish them every day.

Heartfelt thanks to my wife Cherie, whom I adore. She gives me endless support and helps me stay focused on the important things in life. Thank you to my children, Amelia (11 yrs.) and Matthew (9 yrs.), for continually teaching me that anything is possible. I appreciate the opportunity to see the world through the eyes of an innocent child.

And special thanks to my father Frank J. Mannino for demonstrating the principles of being the best a person can be. Every day throughout my entire childhood, his actions taught me how to give without the expectation of receiving. And to my mother, June Mannino, for believing in me and allowing me to pursue my dreams.

Finally, I want to give thanks to GOD for using me as a tool to bear witness for all to see. Thank you for allowing me to see my strengths & giving me the wisdom to realize my full potential. It is through him that *all* things are possible.

Introduction

   Simple Solutions For Selling is a practical solution for business owners, managers & sales staff to compete and succeed in today's demanding world of retail sales. Large corporations are grabbing more and more market share, making it harder for small to medium size businesses to realize their true potential. This book will help build a foundation of knowledge and team spirit for your associates. These simple strategies will focus your sales staff and management team for success and greater profits. The solutions presented in this book were developed to work on today's ever demanding retail sales floor. Any size team, in any market can benefit from applying the sales techniques offered in this book.

   Current economic conditions have forced the retail industry to self-analyze to figure out how to increase their shrinking profits and spend less to compensate. It has become more of a self-serve environment over the past two decades, increasing the independence customers feel while shopping. A great example of this is the "Do It Yourself" mentality that has forever changed the retail sales floor. For example, the hardware industry has changed significantly over the last 20 years. This creates an opportunity that can be exploited by the smaller business owner and used to their advantage. Staff training and customer service standards are two key elements to focus on. These elements will allow you to be more competitive and give you an edge on the competition no matter what size, big or small.

   Would you be happy with a 10% - 15% sales growth? Most retail businesses strive for an average growth of 10%. If your sales team is pursuing their job correctly by asking the right questions and identifying opportunities, this is a modest increase that should happen naturally. Most well established businesses are happy with a modest increase especially during a hard economic time period. In reality the businesses that accept the fact that continuing education for their sales staff will enable them to stand out in their respective markets. The results are a higher return of profit and gain of market share. In addition, your staff will be happier and satisfied with their performance, thus creating a better work environment. Because it is impossible for each individual business owner to create a sales team with individuals as dedicated or as knowledgeable as they are, I created this training manual to guide you in developing and maintaining your staff to produce the best results possible for your business.

Simple Solutions For Selling is presented in chapters that are intended to be used as individual training sessions for your sales staff and management team. Each chapter in the book corresponds with a companion sales or management training module that is available for purchase at *www.SolutionsForSelling.com.* The title of this publication is "**Sales & Management Training Modules: Solutions For Selling**" and incorporates a disc that includes supplemental documents and forms that will help simplify the daily operations of your business. Every document, form or spreadsheet is fully editable and adaptable for your business. A sample of each supplement can be viewed in the "Supplements" section of this book.

These selling ideas and techniques are universal as we break down the selling process into easy to understand sections. These concepts are simple to understand but can be a challenge to learn and execute with consistency. Allow your staff the time needed to digest the information and practice the concepts explored. I recommended not exceeding more than two training sessions per month. This will give your staff a greater level of success as these concepts become habit. Too many concepts in a short time span will limit the learning process and de-motivate your team. Plan well in advance and get your staff excited to further their own success.

What makes a successful business?

Sales Training?   Motivation?
Staffing?   Merchandising?   Location?

I consider these to be the top five categories that require exploration. Each one is very important and can hold the key to expanding your business by leaps and bounds. Let's take a look at each.

I'm sure much thought went into where you ultimately set up shop. It has been said that the top three considerations for a successful business are location, location & location! This element is critical if you are planning on opening up a new store or even if you're going to relocate. You'll need to do your due-diligence to make sure you are where you need to be considering cost analysis, accessibility & building features.

Merchandising is critical to being successful. The larger companies have figured this out a long time ago as they grew and increased their business to grab more of the market share. Your market share! So many single store operators and small chain stores lack a merchandising plan that really works. So what's the answer? Well, every store is different in so many ways. The merchandising guidelines presented in this book will give you the solutions needed to keep you on track.

Staffing is a very misunderstood category by many business owners and managers. This manual will help give clarity through a simple approach that can be understood by all. No experience required, just the heart to want to do your best.

Your management staff has the responsibility to excite your sales staff. It is important to have an understanding of how to initiate a positive attitude to perpetuate the cycle necessary to keep your staff motivated. Management skills are very trainable and so worth the investment of time and energy to prepare them for success.

Never underestimate the power of having your sales team fully trained and ready to reel in the business. Not to be confused with clerking or just ringing up the sale, but rather instituting a selling method that creates opportunities to capitalize on.

So, what does it take to be successful?

Do you need to be excitable to be a successful *salesperson?* **No!**

Do you need to be controlling to be a successful *leader*? **No!!**

Do you need to be "all knowing" to be a successful *business owner*?

No!!!

Let's take a look at what it takes to run a successful business that has a steady increase of customers and profits...

Sales Training

(Chapters 1 thru 10)

Chapter 1

Sales Formula

Part A

The Selling Sequence

*"Minds are like parachutes,
they only work when they're open"*

– David Armstrong

1 - Sales Formula: Part A

This should be a moment of new beginnings. Start fresh with an open mind and allow your thoughts and awareness to focus on the principles presented. Making a commitment to put a system in place is essential for the success of the team and yourself. The adoption of principles combined with your fellow associates will create a synergy for success that will be unstoppable.

Being prepared and being consistent are two essential aspects for a sales person to be successful in any selling situation. An effective salesperson will need a road map to provide direction to reach their destination. This journey can be very exciting. Every transaction or sale is uniquely different and never the same twice.

A framework needs to be established to create an environment to thrive in. This framework is called the "Selling Sequence". This sequence of selling tools can be broken down into seven easy steps that will help you reach your destination. A great sales person will be able to flow naturally through each step with their customer. This process enables a symbiotic bond that gives your customer the confidence to *trust* and *want* to buy from you.

1 - Sales Formula: Part A

The "Selling Sequence":

1. Approach & Develop Relationship

2. Ask Questions & Listen

3. Recommendation & Demonstration
   (offer features and benefits)

4. Ask for the Sale & Close

5. Overcome Objections

6. Repeat Steps 5 & 4
   (as needed to close the sale)

Memorizing each step of the *Selling Sequence* is imperative for every selling professional. Continue to practice with your peers until you are comfortable with each step.

Breaking it down:

1. **Approach & Develop Relationship:** A good sales person will be able to create a natural rapport with the customer from the start. A relationship is important to develop before any selling begins. Trust has to be earned and can't be rushed. Never ask if you can help your customer but rather assume they need advice and communicate in a way that develops the relationship.

1 - Sales Formula: Part A

2. **Ask Questions & Listen:** Asking just the right questions will give you the proper information so that you will be able to make an intelligent recommendation. You need to find out **who, why, what** and **where.** Easily remember able as the four *W's*:

> *Who* is the item for?
>
> *Why* do they need this item?
>
> *What* item are they looking for?
>
> *When* do they need this item?

These questions will only give you the basics toward the information you need.

Always listen. You must pay attention to your customer's answers if you want to have a chance at recommending an item that fits their needs properly. Your customer won't purchase from you if they don't feel heard or think that the salesperson is on their own agenda. Only through listening will you gain perspective of what the customer truly needs and wants.

3. **Recommendation & Demonstration:** After asking the appropriate questions and listening intently, you will be able to make your best recommendation. When demonstrating, keep it brief and easy to understand. Be sure not to oversell the item. Try to only make one recommendation and remember to speak with confidence. Think of yourself as a doctor prescribing critical medication for your patient to be

1 - Sales Formula: Part A

healed! Would you tell your doctor "No, not just yet!" or "I'll think about it"!

Offer *features* and *benefits* when describing the item. These attributes are the basis for what the customer is truly buying. Not just the item but what that item is going to do for the customer. Always remember - *features* and *benefits*.

4. **Ask for the Sale & Close:** The preferred method is the "assume" close. After all they came to your store to buy that item. You should be the one to close the deal. Ask assuming questions like "Which color would you like to take home today?" or "How many would you like to purchase?"

5. **Overcome Objection:** If the customer is not committing to the purchase it is because there is an objection in their mind. It is your job to find out exactly what it is and overcome it. If you've done a good job establishing a relationship, this step will be easier.

6. **Repeat Steps 5 & 4** *(Overcome Objection & Ask for the Sale)***:** Repeat as needed until you overcome the last objection and close the sale. This is so important to understand. How many times do you close the deal on your very first try? Don't be afraid to repeat this step as needed. Some experts claim that the successful salesperson averaged 11 attempts before they were able to close the sale. Usually the more objections you overcome, the more firm the sale. It's all in the relationship that you are able to establish. Don't be shy or afraid to lead the customer in the direction you want them to go.

1 - Sales Formula: Part A

To Be Successful:

• **Know** your **product**. This will give you confidence and help you gain respect from your customer.

• **Assume** they came to **purchase**, not just to look. After all, they are in your store for a reason.

• **Create urgency** for your customer to purchase.

> Example:
> - "This is the last one."
> - "The sale ends soon. "
> - "I think this one is special."
> - "Don't miss out on this great purchase!"

• **Compliment** your customer so they feel special and noticed.

> Example:
> - "This looks good on you."
> - "You have a good eye for this."
> - "You're making a great choice."

• **Hold back** on some features or benefits before asking for the sale. Don't use all of your tools in the sales chest before landing the deal. Be smart and save some features to help close your sale.

1 - Sales Formula: Part A

Example:
- quality ratings
- warranty
- special published reports
- special financing

* **Utilize** other **staff** members when applicable to gain credibility. Some staff members are stronger in certain areas that can be used to your advantage if you need the support.

* **Create** customer **confidence** with your return policy and lowest price guarantee. "Best price you can find on the best gear." Save these until the end and use only when needed to help finalize the deal.

* **Be comfortable** closing the sale. Know several closes you have used in the past that were successful.

Example:
- "Which model would you like to take home?"
- "Can I put this on the counter while you pick out some accessories?"

* **Don't give up**. Keep asking for the sale.
(*see step 7 of the selling sequence*)

1 - Sales Formula: Part A

Make it an *EVENT!!!*

    Be different, let loose, have fun, include others or family members in the selling process. Be tasteful. Gain the respect & trust of your customer. Create a lasting impression and you'll gain a customer for life, making you a winner every time.

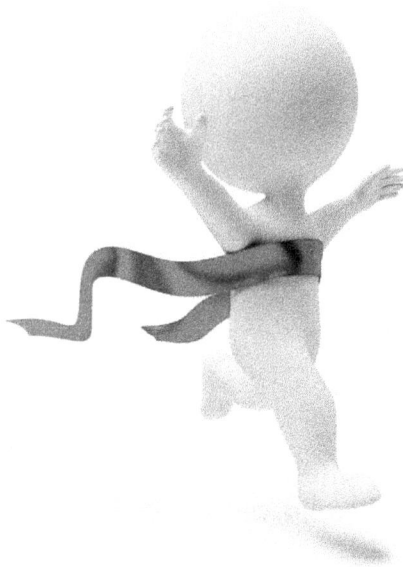

Chapter 2

Sales Formula

Part B

Artistry of the Add-On

*"Do not follow where the path may lead.
Go instead where there is no path
and leave a trail."*

– Ralph Waldo Emerson

2 – Sales Formula: Part B

Selling *add-ons* are one of the crucial components of providing exceptional customer service while maximizing sales and profits in your store. Customers may have a need to buy more items but may not think of it at the right moment. It is our job to recommend specific items or services available for them to purchase. Like casting your bait into the water to attract a big fish!

Artistry of the Add-On

What is an Add-On?

An add-on is anything you sell in addition to the customer's original purchase. There's the obvious and then there's the not so obvious. Your store should have several impulse items that could attract a wide variety of customers. An experienced sales person would be able to provide a wide range of items to add-on and some not so obvious items that your customer would want or could need! You could offer your customer a package that has the intended item inside. This creates a better value for the customer and increased sales for the store. Maybe the add-on turns out to be a larger item than the initial item your customer came in for.

All of our customers have
"needs" and "desires"

2 – Sales Formula: Part B

"Needs" are items that a customer comes into your store looking for. There's a specific need or problem that must be satisfied or solved. It is a salespersons job to resolve these problems by matching the right item to solve the needs of your customer. They typically know what they need but don't always realize or remember their wants. These items are typically blocked by obstacles called objections. These objections need to be identified and overcome.

"Desires" are items that a customer would like to have. They may not know that they need it at that moment but the *want* is there regardless. All desires reside either in the conscious or in the unconscious realm. Most customers have many desires that they realize in the conscious realm but throw up obstacles in their minds that tell them to wait. This could be because of finances or getting an approval from a significant other to purchase the item. The list is endless.

It's the unconscious realm that so many wants are being stored in our brains. They've been created from all of the many lifelong experiences influencing how we think and how we act. Knowing the vast number of wants that are kicking around in our minds should make it easier to see how a salesperson would want to tap into these resources. Each desire can equate to on add-on item. The more add-on items you sell ...well you see the picture.

Why do we sell Add-Ons?

Best customer service & profitability. If your customer gets what they came in for, is this considered a successful sale? You would think so wouldn't you? Well not if they are missing that extra ingredient that would allow their item to work better. Maybe you could include something that would give your

2 – Sales Formula: Part B

customer more pleasure with their original purchase. As an added benefit, this will naturally increase your profitability. In many instances the add-on items will yield much more profit as a percentage to cost than the original item that is being purchased.

When do we sell Add-Ons?

ALL THE TIME! This is easier said than done! Don't miss out on potential add-on sales because you're satisfied just to make the initial sale. You must maintain integrity and quality. Quantity is good but is never a good replacement for quality. Practice by listing several specific situations you can increase your items per transaction. Examples of effectively adding-on to a sale would be demonstrating an impulse item at checkout or recommending a larger size, adding value.

Who do we approach with Add-Ons?

Basically everybody you come in contact with! Really, everybody! There shouldn't be any exceptions. Every sale or even potential sale has an add-on item or several that should be offered to your customer. These opportunities are like diamonds in your backyard waiting to be dug up. All you need to do is ask. Below is a list of selling opportunities.

Large item sale – this is the most common and the easiest. Your customer should need several items to complete the package.

Accessories sale – even if they came in for a small item purchase, it doesn't mean they can't use several other appropriate items that could be offered.

2 – Sales Formula: Part B

Service sale – if you offer a service (repairs, lessons etc...) don't forget to include any other items that will let your customer experience their product to its fullest potential.

How can we be effective with offering Add-Ons?

Get ready to dig in!

✓ Don't rush the sale. Take your time and let the customer know you want to show them what they will need to consider so they may be successful with their new purchase.

✓ Know the product and all of the items needed to best achieve the customer's objective. Practice with role playing. This is a must, unless you are naturally doing these things already. Yeah right!

✓ Discuss these add-on items during the sale. Plant the seeds now and watch them grow. This is necessary to be successful.

✓ Present items to customer with confidence. The customer will trust your professional advice.

✓ Ask the right questions. Find out all of your customers "Needs" and always make recommendations to stimulate their "Desires".

✓ The key to selling add-ons is the relationship that you have established with your customer.

2 – Sales Formula: Part B

✓ Challenge yourself to be better than you are now each and every time you are in front of a customer.

✓ Selling add-ons is considered to be exceptional customer service.

✓ A customer buying a gift for one occasion may also have another upcoming event.

Hey Captain, don't let the big one get away!

Chapter 3

The Customer

*"Never be afraid to try something new.
Remember, amateurs built the ark
and professionals built the Titanic."*

– Anonymous

3 – The Customer

Definition of **"Waiting on a Customer"**: To engage the customer on the sales floor, in conversation, in an attempt to find out information to make appropriate recommendations and suggestions for several appropriate products and/or services from your store.

First Contact!

The single and only opportunity your sales person has to make a good first impression is critical for a retail store and often overlooked by owners and management. Maybe it was addressed in the company manual but not being implemented and since forgotten. Sales are surely lost or created during the initial contact of salesperson and customer. Something so simple can make a huge difference in the percentage of sales to customer count and the overall attitude or vibe that your store portrays.

This method will insure that every customer receives a minimum level of service in your store. Once a customer enters your store, these steps must take place with *every customer, every time.*

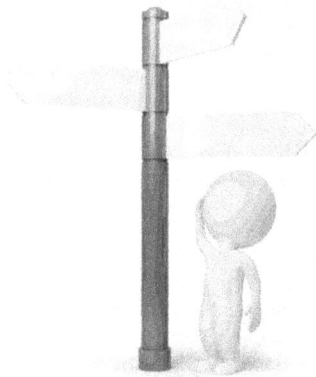

These steps must take place every time we address a customer:

1. Every customer is **greeted** and approached by a salesperson within their initial visit upon entering the store.

3 – The Customer

2. **Communicate** with the customer on the sales floor and not from behind the counter unless you are a dedicated cashier and not a sales person. The cashier should assist in acquiring a sales person to begin the selling sequence.

3. Use an **open ended question** designed to create a discussion between the customer and the employee to help create a relationship. These are questions that require some thought to answer and not just blurt out "OK" or "no thank you".

4. **Express the desire** to want to help your customer with their needs. Trust between the customer and salesperson is earned and should not be taken for granted.

5. **Listen** to your customer's ideas, not just their words. Your response should be concise and on target with their solving their need.

6. Get your customers **involved** in your demonstration. This will promote ownership and a happy ending for the salesmen.

Remember that honesty is paramount to create a relationship that could and should last for a very long time. The goal is to gain a customer for life. Also know that it's not a good idea to correct your customers who use incorrect terms or mispronounce industry jargon.

3 – The Customer

Customer Service

Customer service is a term used by companies very loosely. Some mean it and others talk about it and think that it's happening! Think back to a previous encounter at one of your favorite establishments. How were you treated? Were you comfortable with your surroundings? Did you receive expert advice and was there any follow up involved? Have you ever felt abandoned while you needed help to locate an item? Maybe your surroundings were not comfortable or pleasant to be in. Were you inclined to return? Customers deserve excellent customer service. Businesses that want to excel will need to achieve a level of excellent customer service. This should leave your customer feeling supported and cared for, just like a good relationship. The rapport that is established between you and your customers is also necessary to keep them coming back. Repeat business is like finding golden nuggets in your backyard. Not a bad thing when you think about it!

Too often I visit a retail store, look around and the place is unorganized and filthy. Getting waited on is a stretch and when I do get help, I'm asked "Can I help you?" ...usually by an unhappy and underpaid associate. Now with years of conditioning our customers with a long string of bad salesmen, most customers can't help but to say "No. I'm just looking." Even if their actually needing help! I know human nature plays a part in this phenomenon. Our customers would rather look around and figure it out for themselves instead of asking for help from a sales person. You want to create an environment that will help the selling process and create a level of excellence when serving your customer.

3 – The Customer

After all, who is the customer?

✓ The *Customer* is the most important person in this store or on the phone.

✓ The *Customer* is not dependent on us...we are dependent on them.

✓ The *Customer* is not an interruption of our work...he/she is the purpose of our work.

✓ The *Customer* is not someone to argue or match wits with. Nobody ever won an argument with a Customer!

✓ The *Customer* is a person who brings us his needs and wants. It is our job to handle them as an expert to the advantage for the customer as well as the company.

Remember...

Customers pay our paychecks!

3 – The Customer

Customer Personality Types

Have you ever wondered why you seem to hit it off right away with some customers, while with others it's more like oil and water? That's because we respond intuitively to the natural chemistry, or lack thereof, between temperament styles. Our temperament style not only determines our behavioral traits, body language patterns and buying style, but it also influences our compatibility with other people. If you are able to quickly identify the personality style of the customer, you will know the "how's" and "why's" of what to say to meet their needs. Once they feel that you truly understand them and feel an emotional connection, they will come up with the logical reasons to buy from you.

It's a strategic advantage to identify the personality type of your potential and existing customers. Although every customer is different, most can be grouped into one of four groups:

1. **Analytical** aka **"Thinkers"**

2. **Expressive** aka **"Speakers"**

3. **Passive** aka **"Listeners"**

4. **Dominant** aka **"Doers"**

3 – The Customer

Each of these four primary behavioral styles requires a different approach and selling strategy. What you want to do is identify your customer's personality type and be able to sell your goods and services using your customer's personality to your advantage. In order to be better at what we do and make more sales, you have to understand your customers. Understanding customer personality styles will quickly tell you just how and what to say to each customer.

Now, if you don't feel that you belong to any one group, don't worry, many of us don't fit squarely in one group or another. However, we do have one dominant personality style that we use day to day. Recognizing pros and cons of your specific personality style can help you understand how to better deal with your customers. Listed below are some basic characteristics of each of these personality styles.

1. Analytical – Analytical people are known for being systematic and deliberate. When you give them details, they will analyze and follow them exactly. They like a sales process which is detailed which includes a lot of facts. They like to do a lot of research before they purchase. They appreciate facts and information presented in a logical manner as documentation of truth.

Given that they are detailed orientated they tend to ask a lot of "Why" questions. They will take their time in making a buying decision and will not purchase until they have sufficient facts or proof to justify the purchase they are making is a good decision. Give them evidence, facts, testimonials and guarantees.

Challenges include indecisiveness. They must have ALL the facts before they make a decision. Others could see them as a bit stuffy at times and hard to establish a rapport. They may become irritated easily with glitches. They often get bogged down in detail because they like to avoid making mistakes.

Character traits include:

- orderly   - logical   - persistent   - conventional
- cautious - disciplined - systematic - diplomatic
- serious   - organized   - deliberate   - perfectionist

Tactics for the Analytical:

1. SLOW DOWN! They like to write down everything and make sure they have all the facts.

2. Don't be afraid to give them all of the data they want. The more the better.

3. Be very precise with all of your information.

4. Close the sale with the analytical by reducing their fear of making a mistake.

2. Expressive – The expressive is very outgoing and enthusiastic, with a high level of energy. They are often thought of as a talker, overly dramatic, impulsive, and manipulative. Rapport building is easy. They love to bond with people and get along with EVERYBODY. They are also great idea generators, but usually do not have the ability to see the idea through to completion.

3 – The Customer

The Expressive worry's a lot about what others think and social acceptance is really important to them. They are opposite to the Dominant personality type and ask many "Who" questions. The more visual and *expressive* your presentation, the greater attention you'll receive from your client. They usually prefer a fast paced presentation or sales approach and like to be involved in the process of the sale but are slow to reach a decision.

Challenges include Impatience. They tend to bore easily and detach or move away from a situation to avoid loss of self-esteem.

Character traits include:

- verbal	- motivating	- impulsive	- enthusiastic
- charming	- confident	- dramatic	- optimistic
- animated	- ambitious	- friendly	- stimulating

Tactics for the Expressive:

1. Build a good rapport, but don't visit!

2. Use the customer's name often

3. Emphasize the word "special"

4. Agree with them as much as possible – avoid arguing

5. Sell not only to them, but to their family as well.

3. Passives – Passives are introverts, indecisive, patient and uninvolved – a complete opposite to the expressive. They like a sales process which is much slower paced. They like to connect before talking about business. They hate to be pressured and shy away from conflict.

They ask a lot of "How" questions to be assured that they are making the right decision. They dislike having to make decisions and are natural born procrastinators who love the status quo. They have a tendency to agree with you and stay away from confrontation.

Challenges include wishy-washy. They sometimes cannot make up their mind, needing the approval from other people. Overly-sensitive, their feelings can be hurt easily.

Character traits include:

- willing	- mature	- supportive	- considerate
- loyal	- trusting	- agreeable	- empathetic
- stable	- relaxed	- dependable	- sympathetic

Tactics for the Relater:

1. Use empathy!

2. Always reassure them that their decision is the RIGHT decision.

3. Be very patient and focus on the relationship.

4. Once they commit to the sale, don't waste time.

4. Dominant – Thrives on the thrill of the challenge and the internal motivation to succeed. They are practical folks who focus on getting results and can do a lot in a short time. The impatient and goal-oriented Dominant prefers a quick, bottom line presentation style. They expect you to be on time and well prepared. They like it when you avoid small talk and get right down to business.

Dominants are generally quick to make a decision. They are focused on results and ask "what" questions. They usually talk fast, direct and to the point and often viewed as decisive, direct and pragmatic. Keywords to use when presenting to a Dominant are results, speed and control.

Challenges include inflexible and impatient. "Just the facts..." Tend to be non-empathetic: Intolerant of feelings and inadequacies. Poor listening habits: In one ear and out the other. Never seem to relax: Everything is a competition.

Character traits include:

- decisive	- risk taker	- determined	- action-oriented
- assertive	- practical	- competitive	- strong willed
- stable	- efficient	- independent	- results-oriented

Tactics for the Relater:

1. Establish rapport quickly, but don't try to become friends.

3 – The Customer

2. Keep the presentation moving steadily.

3. Always use the proper title and last name.

4. When you close and get a commitment, GO!

In light of all this, there are many other factors that influence the sale. Just because you know your customers personality type does not guarantee you the sale. What it does guarantee is better communication and in sales you must first understand before you can be understood. With this knowledge, you will be able to tailor your presentations to coincide with your customer's personality profile. Let the customer's personality work to your advantage, not theirs. This leads to more sales and more success.

Chapter 4

Developing a Better
"Selling Attitude"

"It's always better to try a swan dive and deliver a colossal belly flop than to step timidly off the board while holding your nose."

*– Tom Peters philosophy
as described by Fast Company*

4 – Developing a Better Selling Attitude

Because everyone likes to buy, but no one likes to be sold, what you really want to do is simply get your customers to want to buy from you. These training points are lessons on how to find ways to help other people - not to try to sell them, but to gain their confidence and build a relationship. If you want people to buy from you, it's got to be about helping them get what they need. Once you get in the habit of doing this, sales have a wonderful way of happening automatically!

Top Seller

Here are some ways to develop and adjust your selling attitude to become a *"Top Seller"*!

4 – Developing a Better Selling Attitude

• **Constantly work** the sales floor. Never congregate with other salespeople on the sales floor and don't get trapped behind the sales counter or register. This gives the customer a totally different perspective of who their dealing with. To greet a potential customer or client face to face without any barriers between the two aids in building a healthy relationship.

• Be a **good listener** or 'Diagnose before you prescribe'. Salespeople should see themselves as **problem solvers**, and to solve problems correctly, they must first understand the nature of the problem they intend to solve. If you show someone how you can solve their problem, you have a greater chance of making that sale.

• Talk to your customers and **control** the sale. You have the ability to steer the dialog instead of following the current that may lead you over the falls!

• Know your product and be an **educator**. Anytime you can teach effectively - you automatically gain your customers respect and will likely be viewed as the **expert**. People seek out experts, and are more willing to place their trust in them. Master this lesson and watch your sales grow.

• Be someone who **cares**. Always be on the lookout for ways to make a difference for others. Seek a reputation of going the extra mile. This could be as simple as offering a free tips sheet or report, or even helping someone carry a stack of boxes. Or it could be as complicated as volunteering with your local non-profit or networking group.

www.SolutionsForSelling.com

4 – Developing a Better Selling Attitude

◆ Under promise and **over deliver**. Win the hearts of your customers by giving them more than they expect. Never promise what you may not be able to deliver. Go the extra distance and make it happen.

Lessons on how to become a "Top Seller"

1. Be positive and energetic:

   a. Be entertaining with a fun personality
   b. Show enthusiasm about your product
   c. Have excitement for the company you work for
   d. Be willing to go the extra mile
   e. Cultivating leads with follow through
   f. No *personal issues* on the sales floor
   g. Enthusiasm toward all aspects of the store (stats, product, educating public, connecting with public etc...)

2. Motivation:

   a. Hungry to sell; be driven!
   b. Achieve through competition
   c. Monetary vs. personal rewards
   d. Being honest and trustworthy in the customer's eyes

4 – Developing a Better Selling Attitude

3. Goal driven:

    a. Always know your personal sales goal
    b. Conscious of the store forecast and goals
    c. Be aware of company statistics

4. Communication skills:

    a. Approach customers on the sales floor
    b. Learn the customer's name and use it to help develop the relationship
    c. Be a good listener, understanding the needs of the customer
    d. Re-state your customer's objections for clarity of communication
    e. Develop proper timing of the selling sequence
    f. Be able to multi-task (phones, customers, projects etc…)
    g. Communicate effectively with superiors and other staff

5. Product Knowledge:

    a. Be eager to learn (ever expanding knowledge)
    b. Understand the selling sequence *(approach & develop, ask questions & listen, recommendation & demonstration, ask for sale & close, overcome objections, ask for sale & close)*
    c. Practice Add-On, Suggestive, Best Buy, and Solution Selling techniques on the sales floor
    d. Assist others to learn with role playing

    e. Know the quantity levels of stock in your store
    f. Memorize the pricing of your product and your competitor's product

6. Selling Skills:

    a. Ask the right questions, guiding the customer
    b. Feel comfortable to add-on naturally with little effort
    c. Never congregate with other staff members on the sales floor
    d. Extract and cultivate leads from the customer
    e. Avoid walking in the customer's direct path
    f. Concentrate on sales at the right time of day (afternoon, weekend) and not on projects

7. Team Effort:

    a. Be a team player, able to tag team with other associates
    b. Promote greater product knowledge
    c. Create a positive environment to work in
    d. Synergize the staff while promoting store unity

8. Leadership:

    a. Take the initiative to be the best
    b. Be creative and proactive
    c. Look for opportunities to connect and grow
    d. Educate yourself and continue to train
    e. Set the example for others
    f. Have sharp organizational skills (working from lists, maintaining leads in book, materials in proper place etc...)

Taking Ownership

This quality must come from the top and flow down. The owner should instill this quality into the managing staff and support staff. The managing staff should instill this quality into the selling staff.

4 – Developing a Better Selling Attitude

What does Taking Ownership look like?

- Pride & image of one's self
- Values promoted with personal integrity
- Believing in your product & company
- Be a part of the store's success

How is this accomplished?

Your staff needs the opportunity to be a part of the success. This can be accomplished by giving them an area to be responsible for or letting them merchandise a new display. It helps for them to get positive feedback as they work directly with other teammates in a definite project. Your staff should have the opportunity to express themselves and have input that can have a real effect on the stores success.

Chapter 5

Selling Techniques

"There are no rules here -
We're trying to accomplish something"

– Albert Einstein

5 – Selling Techniques

Y ou need to have good tools to do a good job. With the right tools and the right attitude, you can do a great job. We will be focusing on three extremely important techniques. Each one of these techniques is powerful enough to drastically increase your sales and more than double your profitability if practiced correctly. Every sales person should recognize this potential and use these techniques on every selling opportunity as if it were second nature.

"Suggestive Selling" **& "Best Buy Selling"** are two of the most common and important tools in your toolbox. **"Solution Selling" & "Cross Training"** are concepts that will give your staff a high level of confidence. Once you've had a chance to explore these concepts with your staff, sit back and watch the magic happen!

"Suggestive Selling" Technique

Why do we want to *Suggestive Sell*?

- Making good recommendations on items will help our customers get all of the items they need and desire. This is good customer service.

- Suggestive Selling will establish you as the "expert" and will afford you the opportunity to create CFL's (customers for life).

5 – Selling Techniques

• Total sales dollars will significantly increase as a result of effective Suggestive Selling.

• Most accessories purchase can easily be doubled. This is a great tool for increasing your profitability.

• This method will increase your profitability after selling a large ticket item that yielded a lower profit margin. Adding items at a higher profit margin will help the entire sale.

• The salesperson has an opportunity to stand out and potentially make more money depending on the commission structure.

How do you *Suggestive Sell* effectively?

• Energy and enthusiasm are critical to Suggestive Selling. Customers will decide to buy or not based on your excitement about the products that you are recommending. If you are showing tons of excitement about an item the customer will get excited as well. How you present the item through body language and vocal inflection is vital.

• Sell on the sales floor, not at the register. Once a customer has reached the register their buying decisions have been made and suggestive selling is extremely limited. Plant ideas of appropriate items your customer may need early in the selling process. This will enable you to make great recommendations before your customer finalizes a price in their mind of how much they will be spending today.

• Before attempting to Suggestive Sell, establish a rapport and earn the trust of your customer. Greet the customer from the sales floor (not from behind the counter).

5 – Selling Techniques

Positioning in the store is important to customer perception and establishing a non-salesman like appearance.

• Ask questions that require your customer to give answers other than "No thanks. I'm just looking". Start with non-business related questions to build the relationship. Show interest in what they have to say and direct the conversation. Be in charge by asking leading questions with the intent to Suggestive Sell.

• Make good recommendations based on the information you get from asking the right questions. Suggested products must be items that will legitimately benefit the customer. Be prepared by knowing what products are good suggestive items for all types of customers and be able to present the benefits. Keep your skills sharp and be aware of your inventory.

• Use convincing and powerful vocabulary when demonstrating the product. This will help lead your customer in the direction you want to go. Here are some examples: That can *absolutely* be delivered. That looks *fabulous* on you. That matches *incredibly* well.

"Best Buy Selling" Technique

This technique is designed to give the consumer the best product for their needs. This is usually an upgrade product (usually more expensive) resulting in a more profitable sale. Best Buy Selling could also be simply exposing the customer to other options he or she may not have considered. You always want to start with a better quality (usually more expensive) option. Then you will be able to work your way down typically landing on a higher price than if you would have started with a less expensive item and tried to work your way up to a higher quality item.

> # *Keep in mind; everything is too expensive ...until value is attached to it.*

Tips on how to be successful at "Best Buy" selling:

• Ask your customer if you can show them an item that best fits their needs, realizing that the item may be out of their price range. This will allow the consumer to accept an item with more features. If you're having trouble, asking permission on the front end will open the door for you. Example: "If you will allow me to show you my superior model, I will be able to demonstrate all of the features and benefits available for you to consider".

• Always be sincere. You need to demonstrate how much you believe in your product. This is especially important when you are making a suggestion that is more expensive than the customer expected.

5 – Selling Techniques

* Know your product well. Choose wisely what you are going to recommend and have confidence when demonstrating. The consumer will gain trust and have more respect for you if you are knowledgeable in your field of expertise.

"Solution Selling" Concept

Solution Selling is a special approach to sales. Rather than just promoting an existing product, the salesperson focuses on the customer's pain(s) and addresses the issue with his or her offerings (product and services). The resolution of the pain is what constitutes a true "solution".

Good selling involves asking questions to elicit the prospect's needs and desires. You will need to find the appropriate product or service that meets those needs. If good prospecting (qualifying) is done, then the prospect may already be well suited to the product or service and the salesperson simply needs to lead the prospect to act on their desires and needs. A good salesperson is much more knowledgeable about their product or service than the prospect could ever likely be and can offer valuable information and insight to the decision making process.

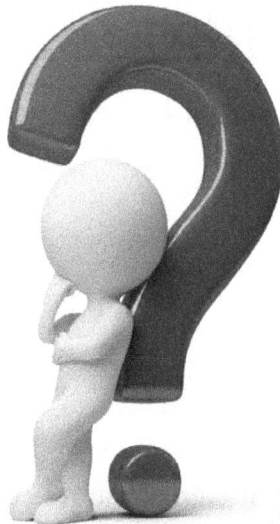

5 – Selling Techniques

"Cross-training" Concept

Every world-class athlete cross-trains. A sprinter lifts weights, runs stairs and even bench presses. If all they did was study and practice sprinting, they may be good, but they would never be great.

Cross-training - According to *Wikipedia*, refers to training in different ways to improve overall performance or the training of one employee to do another's work.

This is an effective technique resulting in motivating everyone involved when properly implemented. Department heads, assistants and employees can cross-train in different departments or within the department itself. Cross-training should be carefully planned and presented as a learning opportunity. Be careful not to implement a "job enrichment" program in a misguided manner, adding unrewarded responsibilities to everyone. This results in a feeling of exploitation and has the reverse of the intended effect.

Every salesperson should have knowledge of each area of the store to be fully trained. This concept will strengthen the entire team from a knowledge point of view. It creates a supportive team that will function stronger from each team member.

Sending people to work in another department at a moment's notice is not what cross-training is about. This has to be an effective planned process. Employees must "buy" into the idea, be encouraged to give feedback and make suggestions for improvement. Examine your staff's knowledge base and determine who is proficient in which areas of the store. You can have your staff train each other as long as it is monitored and measured. A good salesperson will take pride in demonstrating their knowledge and could be used in a training session to lead a topic of interest.

Cross-training can also be used to "shake up" supervisors or employees who have lapsed into poor performance. Upon being moved to a different position or department, albeit temporarily, they hear "warning bells", shape up and usually return to their positions as exemplary performers.

Cross-training achieves the following objectives:

- ✓ Prevents stagnation & rejuvenates all departments

- ✓ Offers a learning and professional development opportunity

- ✓ Improves understanding of the different departments and the business as a whole

- ✓ Leads to better coordination and teamwork & erases differences and unhealthy competition

- ✓ Increases knowledge, skills and work performance

- ✓ Leads to the sharing of organizational goals and objectives

- ✓ Improves overall motivation

Cross-training creates a team of workers who are more knowledgeable, can easily replace each other when needed and who gain new confidence regarding their professional expertise.

Chapter 6

Closing the Sale!

"Until you try,
You don't know what you can do"

– Henry James

6 – Closing the Sale!

What makes a successful sales person?

* Is it being a great persuader? NO, absolutely not! The aggressive salesperson often loses sight of really good customer service and the importance of making sales that stick and cultivates repeat customers.

* How about being in the right place at the right time... Not really, only works sometimes. We all have moments when we walk into a nice sale or two, but will never replace consistency.

* Working the better shifts? Wrong again. This will only allow the average salesperson to do better by default. A gifted sales person will have the ability to create and find opportunities to be successful.

6 – Closing the Sale!

The successful salesperson will consistently rise to the top as they demonstrate the following attributes:

Technique, knowing their craft of successful selling,

Desire to genuinely help people,

Drive to compete and be the best,

Passion to work with people and network,

Adaptive ability to connect with various customers,

Flexibility to work in different environments,

....and of course,

Closing with the consistency of a driven champion.

The *close* of a sale is usually described as the point where your customer agrees to make a purchase. The goal is to book sales that truly help satisfy the customer, and creates a mutually-beneficial, long-term relationship. If you are closing a sale you are tying it all together. It may not work the first time or even the fifth time. You just need to keep overcoming the objections until it is done.

What makes a sale complete? It is when you no longer need to close because the buyer has committed to the sale. You get the buyer to commit to small yeses and ultimately the final yes is a commitment to purchase. It is important to gauge where your customer is in terms of mindset, remove obstacles through answering objections and to serve your client's needs. If your wish is to have a long-term and mutually beneficial

6 – Closing the Sale!

relationship, your goal should be to provide your customer with products and services that will make them successful.

The sales professional must ask for the sale in order to facilitate its successful closure. Asking for the sale can be direct or indirect. The best salesmen are comfortable and proficient with closing the sale using several different techniques. Here is a list of the most common type of closings with examples to study and learn.

Must Know Closes

- ✓ **Direct Close -** Simply ask for the order. You may surprise yourself with how easy it is.

    "Is this the one for you?" / "When would you like delivery?" / "Can I bring it up to the counter while you look around?" / "Would you sign this order form please?" / "May I confirm your delivery and invoice addresses are correct for this order?"

- ✓ **Assume Close -** Making the assumption the customer has made the decision to buy. The sales person will tell them what they are going to do to complete the sale.

    "Let me put that on the counter while you pick out some accessories to complete your purchase."

- ✓ **The Either/Or Close -** Much like the Assume Close but introduces the possibility of a choice. This is a great way to get affirmation from the customer. We're always looking for YES responses.

6 – Closing the Sale!

"Would you like red or green?" / "Would you like this one or one in a box?"

✓ **The Add-On Close -** To focus on an add-on item as the reason to close the deal assuming the customer has made the decision to buy. This requires the salesperson to have developed a good relationship before attempting this technique with success.

"Would you like one of these gadgets to go with your purchase?"

✓ **The Strong Close -** Used to 'strong arm' a prospect after they request something.

"Will you go ahead if we can provide that?"

✓ **Turn Over Close -** You make a list or table of positive and negative points, then take each negative in turn and convert it.

"Yes, it does look expensive, I agree, but if you take into account the durability/reliability/performance, then over time this is actually a much more affordable option."

✓ **Puppy Dog Close -** A method of selling or closing a deal whereby you let the customer try the product or service for free without commitment, for a limited period, in the confidence that once they live with it they won't want to give it up - just like giving someone a puppy for a day.

"Please, take this one home with you tonight. I will call you tomorrow to see how well it performed for you."

What is your favorite "Close" technique?

Cultivating Repeat Business

How are you cultivating repeat business or are you doing anything at all to ensure that your customers are ecstatic about your store. Ultimately, they should want to come back repeatedly and tell their friends all about the great experience they had at your wonderful establishment. A happy customer is a pleasure to have, but an ecstatic one is even better. When you go above-and-beyond to nurture your customers, they will become a reliable source for repeat business and new customers. They'll refer new customers to you, and publicly reinforce your reputation to others over and over again.

So how do you turn those ordinary customers into CFL's – Customers for Life? All it takes is a little understanding of their wants and needs, and some creative strategies for exceeding their expectations. Here are 10 ways to create CFL's that will give your store the word-of-mouth marketing that your business needs to succeed.

6 – Closing the Sale!

1. Anticipate Your Customer's Future Needs

Your customers have a specific idea of what they want but they may not see all the options they have available to them. Talk with them and get a feel for exactly what their needs are and what it is they are trying to accomplish, and offer them advice or services that will make it easier for them to achieve their goals. If applicable, connect them with people who can help make those things happen. Open their eyes to how they can get all of their needs met by using you and your services. They won't forget how valuable it is to keep doing business with you.

2. Present Your Products In Terms of Value

Keep in mind that your customers are basing their decision on how they will personally benefit from their purchase. It's not all about the features. The best way to solidify your sale is to present your products in terms of value. Let them know what they are getting and how it benefits them. This will give a greater value to their purchase and your customers will feel their money is well spent. Everything is too expensive until value is attached to it.

3. Customize Your Approach to Their Problem

Learn as much as you can about what has been preventing your customers from getting the results they want, and customize your approach to highlight how you are the perfect solution. Instead of a typical "here are our services" pitch, present yourself in a way that will make them notice and say "This is exactly what we've been looking for!"

4. Create a Guide That Positions You as An Authority

Being seen as an authority is a powerful way to deliver a "wow-factor" to your customers that increases their desire to stay loyal to you (as well as the amount of business they bring your way). Creating a companion guide to your products or services is an excellent way to showcase your experience and to establish your position as a company who is on the leading edge. Just one more perk of doing business with you and your store.

5. Offer a Workshop or Clinic That Gives You the Edge

Specialty stores arrange periodic clinics to help educate customers on how their products can be beneficial. Home improvement stores offer free do-it-yourself workshops to give customers a reason to shop at their store. Financial planners offer free investment seminars to educate clients on additional products they offer. Your business could do the same. Look at what it is that you sell, and consider the knowledge gaps your customers might have when it comes to choosing options or getting the most out of what they buy. Then offer a free workshop or clinic that closes the knowledge gap, and see just how much more your customers appreciate you.

6. Under-Promise and Over Deliver
. . . every chance you get!

The best way to make a great impression in your customer's mind is simply to exceed their expectations, every chance you get. Don't over-promise, be realistic when telling them what you'll deliver and when they should expect it. Then go the extra mile to make your deliverable impressive and on time (or better yet, early). This is an easy way to virtually guarantee a stream of revenue from your current clients, and the clients they will be referring to the store in the future.

7. Reward Customer Loyalty

Keeping clients long-term saves you the time and money of hunting down new ones, so why not pass some of that savings on to them? Offering clients some sort of bonus or discount periodically, just for sticking with you, is a sure way to impress. Whether you choose to give a discount, or you throw in a free product or service here and there, these unsolicited gifts will make your clients hard-pressed to go elsewhere. Be careful not to go against any company policies. This kind of practice will need to be approved by management if it isn't a standard practice with your company. Also beware not to give the impression you routinely give away your profits. If this technique is done correctly, your customer will respect the service you are providing.

8. Master the Art of Accessibility

One of the easiest ways to consistently impress your customers is to keep your turnaround time on emails and phone calls to a minimum. In today's world of poor customer service, having a quick response rate to customer inquiries is a powerful way to keep them impressed and away from the competition. A quick tip on email – even if you can't address a client's needs immediately, reply to them and let them know you'll get back to them soon. Reinforcing their feeling of being valued gives them another to be a *customer for life.*

9. Keeping Your Customer in the Loop

There will be times that things can take longer than expected. Special orders not arriving on time or even if a project is taking longer than expected, customers appreciate receiving an update with a new ETC (*estimated time of completion*). A simple phone call can set your customers mind at ease. Nobody likes to be left behind in the dark.

10. Ask For Feedback after the Sale

A typical business follows up only when they have something to sell, but you can secure your clients by following up with a thank you note mailed to your customer with a personal note. A simple phone call that follows up with the question "Is there anything we missed, or anything more we could do to make your experience better?" tells your customers that you're 110% committed. Make sure that your customer is treated fairly and respectfully – and that you're not going to settle for letting them get anything less than the best from you.

The underlying theme is to give before expecting to receive. Strong customer relations are the best asset any company can have. Problems or obstacles will always arise – it's the customer relationships that we forge to help overcome those problems. This will help us see difficult situations through to success. These techniques will also increase personal fulfillment by creating those win-win ideas and circumstances. Why can't everybody profit – customers and your store?

Each and every one of these examples can apply to all aspects of the business world. It's all about building relationships that last, because those relationships will bring new ones that last just as long.

6 – Closing the Sale!

Techniques you should continue to work on:

1. Asking for the sale and closing the deal.

2. Completing the sale with additional items (add-ons).

3. Creating repeat customers, getting them to want to return.

4. Getting more leads for future sales and add-ons.

5. Continuing to analyze any missed opportunities.

6. Demonstrating a superior attitude with your colleagues.

Chapter 7

Building Relationships

"Success begins with self-acceptance"

– Fortune Cookie

7 – Building Relationships

Networking

There are two types of networking that will be discussed in this module, *"Inside Networking"* and *"Outside Networking"*. The process of creating business connections on the sales floor using your existing customer base is called *inside networking.* If you are concentrating on attracting new business from approaching organizations or other external sources, it would be considered *outside networking.* Everyone you meet is connected to another person or more likely several people that could benefit from your services or products. Leave no stone unturned by keeping in mind that everyone you meet can either become a prospect, a client, or a friend. These connections are called leads and are used to enhance your personal customer base, thus enhancing the store's total customer base.

Effective and steady sales prospecting is the foundation for every successful sales person. Top performing sales professionals know that they must prospect for new sales leads on a regular basis in order to fill their funnel to create consistent sales. Without this constant effort, a sales person will struggle to achieve their goals. Lead generation will allow the sales person to always have new opportunities for them to sell to.

The Lead Funnel

The following is an illustration for a lead filter, also called the "Lead Funnel". The majority of the leads that are put into the funnel are called Surface Leads. These are mostly "cold" prospects that are theoretically placed into the "Lead Funnel". As you follow-up, many leads won't yield anything and must be filtered out. The remainders of the leads are called Substance Leads ("warm" prospects] because they have the potential to become a Selling Lead or a sale. A Selling Lead is a super "hot" prospect that only needs to be closed. Organize your leads using the "Lead Sheet" (current leads, supplement 9) and "Lead Tracker" (older leads, supplement 10). You will want to strive to reach minimum lead quota on a daily basis.

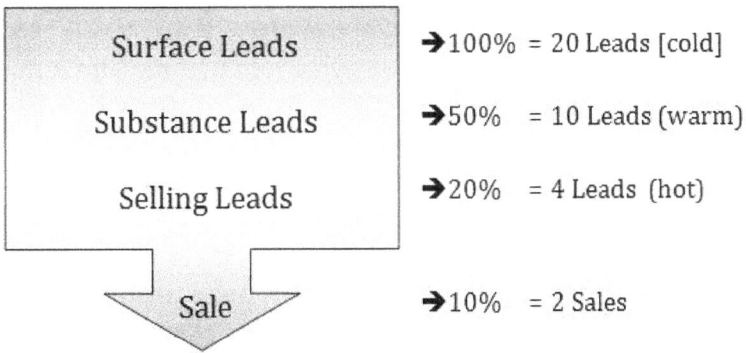

Surface Leads	➜100% = 20 Leads [cold]
Substance Leads	➜50% = 10 Leads (warm)
Selling Leads	➜20% = 4 Leads (hot)
Sale	➜10% = 2 Sales

"Outside" networking requires the ability to cultivate and maintain meaningful relationships with other professionals in your community. These relationships drive sales and foot traffic into your store. A strategic approach to developing a system to help build relationships is necessary so that you don't miss out on the many opportunities that networking can provide.

7 – Building Relationships

How to Approach and Build the Right Relationship:

- ✓ **Be Positive** - Good feelings are contagious and infectious.

- ✓ **Be Confident** - You are not soliciting; you are providing a valuable service to the community. Look people in the eyes when you speak to them. Focus as if he or she is the only person in the world.

- ✓ **Be Friendly** - You are the face for your company. Be professional and congenial in your actions and demeanor.

- ✓ **Be Attentive** - You need to be sensitive to any time restrictions or responsibilities your contact may have.

- ✓ **Be Helpful** - Never show up empty handed or without purpose. Your goal is to become the local trusted professional they can depend on.

- ✓ **Be Proactive** - Anticipate your customers' needs and provide that extra value that is outside of the expected products and services.

- ✓ **Be Yourself** - The opportunity to participate in this activity is a privilege and is arguably the best way to promote your business.

7 – Building Relationships

Recommendations to Build Relationships:

1. Finding new relationships:

   a. Chamber of Commerce

   b. Local Organizations

   c. Private Groups

   d. Associations or Clubs

   e. Church Groups

   f. Competitor Business

2. Fix an existing relationship: This could be just a simple misunderstanding that could yield an untold amount of business!

3. Visit local associations and attend business meetings to gain acceptance and make contacts to network.

4. Build relationships by immediately thanking those who have referred you. If my customer refers me to someone, I'll call and write that referral ASAP. Then I'll go back and thank my customer and let them know that I've made contact and will keep them posted.

7 – Building Relationships

5. Networking is about relationships and the results that happen. When you cultivate people into your life, you'll reap rewards both professionally and personally. They both take time and are worth it.

6. Make lists. Keep a list of your strengths and skills that you can use to prospect. Review it monthly and update it. They might include: great follow up, sending personal notes and emails, or having a friendly attitude. Whatever they are, keeping improving them.

7. Business cards are treasures. When you receive one, treat each one as a possible "closed deal" worth thousands of dollars. It represents the person with whom you're trying to connect.

www.SolutionsForSelling.com

Chapter 8

Is Your Store
Merchandised? Really!

"We are what we repeatedly do. Excellence, therefore, is not an act but a habit"

– Aristotle

8 – Is Your Store Merchandised? Really!

This is a basic overview of principles on how to merchandise and maintain your store. Why do we need to be so concerned with the appearance of our store? Customers are very impressionable. Your store will get judged as soon as customers walk up to the front door. The first impression is critical and could make the difference between just having a chance to demonstrate your products and winning over a customer for life. A well merchandised store will attract customers to your store and the opposite will detract customers. Care for your store as if it were your home. Don't let basic needs like periodic cleaning or touch-up painting go unnoticed.

What does your store look like right now?

You want to allow your staff, as well as your customers, the ability to function with ease inside the store. Yes, even your customers. The store layout, signage and product placement needs to be as easy as possible to understand. Simplicity is the key, as if you were setting up a self-serve environment. Not that you want your customers helping themselves without the assistance of sales staff. There will be times that your staff won't be able to get to everybody. A well merchandised store should be able to accommodate those extra customers during the busy times with ease. Smart merchandising practices will help you keep a clean, good looking store even when your store is at its busiest.

8 – Is Your Store Merchandised? Really!

Top Five Mistakes to Correct ASAP:

1. Pricing incorrect or missing resulting in frustrated customers.

2. Product not consistently merchandised in horizontal lines.

3. Empty pegs on the wall showing an empty product home.

4. Product should always be at the front tip of the peg.

5. Not cleaning the floors, corners, vents in ceiling, restroom etc...

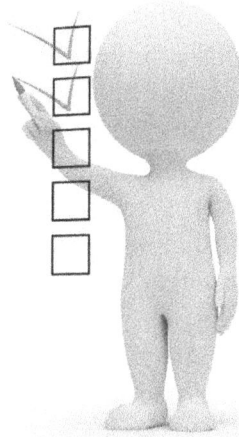

To understand the methodology of Merchandising we need to break it down into sections. First we need to look at what all goes into creating the store appearance that will be acceptable for you. And then we need to consider the structure of how and where to place your product inside the store.

Store Appearance:

A. Front Store Image (Signage, Window Displays etc...)

Big is better when it comes to making an impression with a window display. This analogy also works for store signage and posters displayed in windows and on the building.

8 – Is Your Store Merchandised? Really!

Many retailers make the mistake of creating signage that can't be seen from a distance. If you are presenting posters, they should be hung at the same height in each window (unless going for a special effect). You may want to consider a policy not to hang anything that doesn't fit corporate policy or not to allow anything that isn't professionally produced. Never use visible tape to hang a sign or a general notice on a window or wall. Always find a method that is neat and clean. Consider hooks with suction cups and hanging when possible or two sided tape that is unnoticeable when used.

Store hours should be posted at the entrance for customers to view. Product displays visible through the front windows need to be facing out (towards the outside) and price tags should not be visible. You want to generate interest and create a chance to have a dialog without having to defend the price. Remember that the front of the store must remain clean.

B. Inside Store Presentation (General Layout)

The goal is to have an easy and natural flow that will invite and guide your customers through the various departments or different categories. Consideration for a congruent order is necessary before placement of your product. These departments should stay consistent without very much movement. Your customers will learn the flow of your store and will become accustomed to it. Only change the store flow when you know that the return will be in your favor considering the time, expense and resources you will need to expend.

8 – Is Your Store Merchandised? Really!

You want to appeal to each of the four human senses; sight, sound, touch and smell. Proper merchandising will give your customer a satisfaction in all four areas, so each of them should be addressed.

1. **Sight:** is typically where you will begin to make a first impression. The eyes want to see clean lines and pleasing colors. Creating a store image with clean lines is explained in depth later in the product display section of this module.

2. **Sound:** Don't let this sense go unnoticed. Appropriate music playing in the background can have an influential impact on your customers buying decisions. Also consider the different moods you can create that will have an effect during the different parts of the day. The morning may require something more subtle than the afternoon or even during the weekend. Try to match the mood of your customer and create an environment that you want for your customers that is conducive for shopping.

3. **Touch:** The more you can engage your customers the better effect you can have on their decisions. Working displays or product that can be touched will always help sell your items. The feeling of ownership is enhanced when you are able to hold the item that is being considered. Your customer needs to be able to envision themselves enjoying the many benefits that the item has to offer.

4. **Smell:** Smell is powerful and can be used to your advantage. The wrong smell can also have a powerful effect as well. Sometimes it's hard to tell if you have an

odor problem because you're always in that environment. Samples that smell good are great at attracting a crowd but if your merchandise doesn't have a scent then the best practice is to have a fresh clean smell. Never cover up an unpleasant odor with chemicals or cheap scents as these tactics usually offend a large percentage of people anyway and never solves the problem at hand.

C. Product Displays
(Wall Promotions, Island Display, End Cap Display, Glass Case)

Change is good and expected. Customers want to see featured items and need to be presented with new ideas to keep their interest for continued shopping in your store. Repeat business is vital for a healthy store. You'll want to foster this tactic every chance you get.

Product Merchandising:
(Displayed product throughout the store)

Who's responsible? These are guidelines for the entire staff, not just management to set up and expect to work like magic. Everybody needs to be knowledgeable in the art of merchandising so that maintenance is a breeze.

The creativeness of your staff can also take part in deciding the proper presentation. These concepts are not difficult but rather very logical. Not every product scenario will fit into these guidelines but should be used as closely as possible for the best impact to sell your product.

8 – Is Your Store Merchandised? Really!

✓ Hanging merchandise displays should be sectioned into 4' to 6' (max) areas. Even on a long continuous wall.

✓ Product must be placed in clean horizontal lines beginning from the top left corner and ending at the lower right corner. Each section will also need to have a straight clean line on each side (left & right) of your display.

✓ Product assortment should be consistent representing distinct categories and placed within the product sections without any visual gaps.

✓ The height of the top row of product should not be placed out of reach from your customers. When displaying different sized packaging in one area, consider using a medium to large sized packaging on the top row and possibly the lowest row. Smaller packaging should be merchandised on the center rows closer to eye level.

✓ The strike zone for product merchandising is considered to be at your customer's eye level. This product should be items that you want the customer to consider first because of profitability margins or high impact.

✓ Try never to place small packaged items within the bottom two feet of your display and never put boxed product on the floor without a platform to showcase your items. There should be very few exceptions to this rule.

✓ If products have stickered pricing, they must be easy to understand and accurate.

✓ Pricing stickers must be placed consistently in a uniform place like the top right corner or on the back, lower corner. Avoid covering up any important information that the customer would need to see. (For example: model number, sizing etc.)

Tips:

* Have the tools necessary to correct poor packaging. Extra plastic hanging tabs or adjustable plastic loops can fix missing or distressed packaging.

* Staff should consistently monitor stock that is not being replenished leaving holes in your merchandised product. These gaps can be a visual distraction if left for any substantial length of time. Consider rearranging in a simplistic way to conceal these gaps.

* Product should be fronted to the edge of your merchandising peg consistently through the selling day. Delegate sections of the store to specific staff members. Eventually this should be a natural habit for your employees.

* Consistency of product for customers to be able to know where to go to find the items they need. Try not to change the overall category layout once you have established a system that works for your business.

Every morning you will want to walk your store to determine items to put onto your action list. This needs to be a consistent routine performed by management or the active person in charge.

8 – Is Your Store Merchandised? Really!

→ Items needing re-stocking

→ Misplaced items

→ Displays in need of cleaning

→ Missing price stickers / tags

→ Light bulbs to be replaced

→ Countertop fixtures needing restocking

→ Register supplies

→ Fingerprints on glass cases

→ Clean front door & windows

→ Merchandise displayed poorly

→ Missing or mismatched signage

→ Selling floor displays needing re-stocking

Own Your *Zone*!

Once you have your store picture perfect, you'll want to keep it that way. This is a very effective way to maintain your store and keep that sharp image needed to wow your customers. The "Own Your Zone" program will organize your staff members and assign them sections of the store to maintain on a periodic schedule.

The **Daily "To Do" List** (supplement 4) organizes everyone by department. It will log the progress of each day that the specific task was accomplished. You should rotate the areas between your staff members so that they are all familiar with the different sections of the store. This will help cross train your sales staff. Besides, who wants to clean the restroom over and over! The *"Daily To Do List"* also spells out the end of evening duties for your closing staff. Responsibility starts with organization and having the structure in place will allow your crew to function smoothly thereby allowing for greater stability.

Chapter 9

Telephone Techniques

"You can have anything you want if you are willing to give up the belief that you can't have it"

– Robert Anthony

9 – Telephone Techniques

For many customers, the telephone is the first contact they will have with a business and you never get a second chance to make a first impression. The phone is a valuable tool that can open the door for many opportunities. We must use these skills each time we answer the phone.

Basic Telephone Skills:

1. **Before you answer** --- Take a deep breath and then recite your company's greeting with clarity and not rushed.

2. **Smile, Smile, Smile** --- If you are smiling when you are talking on the phone it will be hard to sound uncaring or uninterested. This is an easy way to insure that your tone is happy and enthusiastic while addressing a customer on the phone.

3. **Answer with enthusiasm and excitement!** --- Build that relationship with a positive start. Customers will want to talk with you and buy from you if you are enjoying what you're doing.

4. **Always answer within 3 rings** --- This is extremely important. Have you ever called a business and had to endure too many rings before the sales person picked up the phone? Then you can understand the customers feeling of frustration. This is an opportunity to demonstrate to the customer that you will be there for them. A critical component that will build trust from the beginning.

5. **Speak slowly and clearly** --- This is a common mistake for a new salesperson that is nervous. The idea is not to throw obstacles at the customer. Ask another salesperson to listen to you as you speak to a customer on the phone. You may be surprised.

6. **Inflection is infectious** --- The proper inflection in your voice can excite your customer and make them want to learn more about your products and services. The wrong inflection can cause them to call elsewhere. Just because they called does not mean that they have decided to do business with you. It is up to YOU to convert the caller into a customer.

7. **Listen to your caller** --- Allow your customer to express what they are looking for so that you can answer their questions properly. Don't let your customers rot on the phone. No silence periods!

8. **Use their name** --- If your caller gives their name remember it and use it. It will impress them and make the call more personal. Have confidence when talking to your customer.

9. **Ask the right questions** --- Don't be afraid to dig deep in order to find out what your customer is asking for. Training and experience will help you to determine the right questions to ask. Capture their name and number for a lead. You can never have too many leads!

10. **Give good answers** --- Remember your goal is to turn them into a customer. Always promote what you have and can offer them. Be sincere when trying to solve your customer's problem.

9 – Telephone Techniques

11. Mention a current promotion --- Know what you're going to say and take the opportunity to entice your customer with a promotional offer.

12. Invite them into the store --- A simple invitation like "Come see me" or "How about this afternoon at 7:00PM" will give the customer the feeling of obligation and the that you want to help them if an appointment time is set, you can be certain that you have your best chance of seeing that customer in your store.

13. Avoid giving prices over the phone --- If the item can be compared to a competitor's product, avoid giving specific prices... give a price range, then take control of the conversation by asking questions. The competitor may have a similar but inferior product that may sell cheaper. Your goal is to get them into your store and convince them to buy from you. If you steer the conversation in the right direction price will not be a factor.

14. Avoid placing on hold --- It's never good to let a customer sit on hold. If you have to, ask their permission and return immediately. If you do not have an immediate answer for your customer again ask their permission to get their name and number so you can get an answer for them and most importantly be sure to **call them back quickly!** If it is a simple transfer to another store member, be sure to monitor the length of time the customer is waiting on hold.

15. Create urgency --- If possible, provide a reason to get them to take immediate action. You want to create urgency for that customer to make the decision to come into the store.

Example: Sale price, low inventory, choice of color etc...

16. ALWAYS thank them for calling --- Before hanging up ask if they know where we you located and ALWAYS thank them for calling.

The phone is never a distraction,

....but an OPPORTUNITY!

Remember: Answer questions properly, solve problems quickly, and give your caller a reason to stop calling the competitors. Convince them to do business with YOU, and they will become your customer!

The Phone Challenge:

The Phone Challenge Worksheet can be found in the supplement section #6. It should be used as a training guide but also as an evaluation tool administered by a secret shopper. The shopper will rate the sales person on the following ten topics:

1. Greet customer properly using company script.

2. Establishing a relationship through dialogue.

3. Find out who the item is for.

4. Make appropriate recommendation.

5. Add-on or up sale attempted.

6. Mention current sales promotion.

7. Identify a networking opportunity.

8. Get the lead (name and phone number).

9. Invite customer to the store.

10. Was the sales person enthusiastic?

This can give you insightful information about how your customers are being treated when they call on the phone. Your image in many instances will start with a phone call. How well you handle these calls will determine if they even come into your store. How many customers are you turning away without realizing it? How many sales opportunities did your staff miss because they didn't ask the right questions or any questions at all? Take the challenge and set up a fun game of secret shopper. Announce your findings at a store meeting and award prizes for those that demonstrated excellence and continue training your staff with average and below average results.

Chapter 10

A Healthy Store

"Success is a science;
if you have the conditions, you get the result"

– Oscar Wilde

10 – A Healthy Store

Expectations / Accountability / Execution!

What is your role as a professional sales person? Are you meeting the minimum expectations? Are you accountable to your supervisor and supporting staff? Are you doing what it takes to rise to the top? These are questions you need to ask yourself daily. Truth is, your supervisor is doing just that! The bottom line is "Taking Ownership". When you have a team that is contributing with pride and integrity as if they owned the business, well then you've got something.

Establishing expectations from the beginning will set the boundaries for your staff to perform at a high level of accountability. Personal success is driven by the consistency of good work ethics, promoting the kind of sales execution you want to see on your sales floor. When you can get your entire sales team to believe in their individual abilities as a professional sales associate and evoke a synergistic esprit de corps (team work), then you've got something to be proud of, something unstoppable.

10 – A Healthy Store

Here are some key points to keep you staff focused on the important aspects of being a professional salesperson.

A. Attitude / Confidence:

1. Demonstrates a positive attitude in the store and with customers.

2. Motivated to go beyond your sales goals.

3. On a quest for training opportunities for continued improvement to be your best.

4. Displays a level of confidence when dealing with customers, giving a sense of authority or ownership.

5. Works well with staff as a team (including all departments)

6. Relates with all types of customers in a genuine manner.

B. Sales Goals / Lead Development:

1. Always know your personal sales goal and stats.

2. Always know your store and company sales goal and stats.

10 – A Healthy Store

3. Cultivates the minimum number of leads required per company standards and logged with appropriate notes taken.

4. Consistent follow up written in lead book (within 48 hours).

5. Exceeding sales goal minimum of 9 out of 12 months.

6. Developing a repeat customer base and actively finding more customers to sell to. *(Networking)*

C. **Salesmanship:** Approach, Listening, Suggesting & Closing

1. Demonstrates a natural rapport with customers.

2. Practicing good selling habits, asking the right questions, selling more stuff.

3. Consistency of approaching your customer.

4. Fluent with the "Selling Sequence" and able to teach it to other staff members.

5. Actively using sales techniques (Suggestive Selling, Best Buy, etc...) to increase personal and store sales.

6. Using your lead book to close more deals.

7. Aware of the higher profit margin items in your store.

8. Identifying and taking advantage of opportunities.

D. Networking Opportunities:

1. Know all of your competition in your area.

2. Attract new business to the store.

3. Aware of the local businesses in your area.

4. Develop relationships with new contacts and organizations.

5. Know all clubs or groups within a 15 mile radius.

E. Operational:

1. Company procedures are followed per established guidelines.

2. Paperwork is properly filed and handled with a minimum amount of touches allowing for greater efficiently.

3. Using the "Own Your Zone" checklist (supplemental 4] to maintain store order and cleanliness keeping it in perfect order.

4. Office supplies and tools are organized and returned to their proper station.

5. Following through on projects, bringing your task to a completion.

6. Being a team member supporting the entire process.

How to Be the Best You Can Be:
A personal "To Do List"

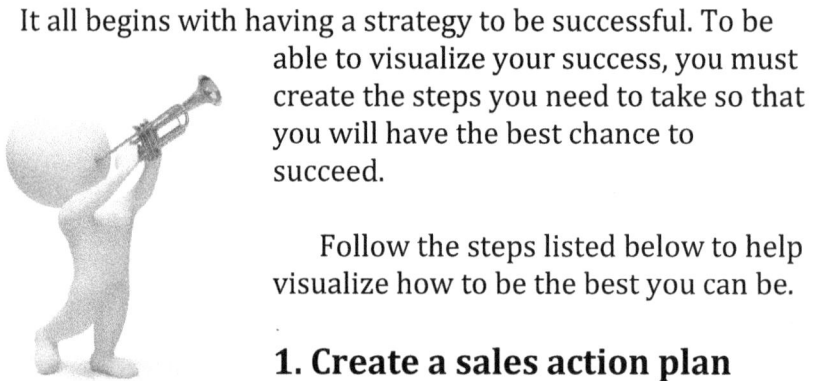

It all begins with having a strategy to be successful. To be able to visualize your success, you must create the steps you need to take so that you will have the best chance to succeed.

Follow the steps listed below to help visualize how to be the best you can be.

1. Create a sales action plan

* Make a commitment to be the best possible

* Write down objectives and review regularly

* Stay positive and be creative

* Focus and compete against your numbers and others around you.

* Be versatile and quick to react

2. Establish personal goals (tangible & obtainable)

* Establish a "dollars per week" & "monthly" goal
* Increase number of "units" sold
* Sell more add-ons per transaction
* Pick an item to sell more of. Make it a quest

3. Identify sales opportunities (think outside the box)

* Be in the right place at the right time
* Ask the right questions to get the information you need
* Continue to build relationships for continued growth
* Network with all of your customers

4. Find new business

* Create an event or clinic
* Consider your competitions customer base
* Locate groups or clubs to attract business (churches, professional organizations, etc...)
* Internet searches for (clubs, groups, etc...)

A list of expectations is only a list of expectations. You'll need to throw it in the pot with accountability and execution to cook up something that will surely satisfy your need to be the best sales person you can be.

VISION
MARKETING
PROACTIVE
PLAN
SOLUTION
BUSINESS
MANAGEMENT
ANALYSIS

What are you waiting for?

Go get'em!

Management Training Tools

(Chapters 11 thru 18)

Chapter 11

Leadership Lessons

"A leader takes people where they want to go. A great leader takes people where they don't necessarily want to go, but ought to be"

– Rosalynn Carter

11 – Leadership Lessons

According to Wikipedia, **Leadership** has been described as the "process of social influence in which one person can enlist the aid and support of others in the accomplishment of a common task". Leaders also have the capacity to build shared values and the desire to reproduce themselves.

People skills are important and very difficult to accomplish. They require leaders to have the ability to listen and be able to develop the capacity to articulate. Leaders are also required to handle emotions without anger and have the ability to treat people with respect. Leaders are flexible and resilient. They realize that pressure is external and that anxiety is the internal reaction to pressure which is either real or anticipated.

Leaders see the big picture,
while managers have the skills
to make the big picture a reality.

11 – Leadership Lessons

Listed below are some important lessons that will focus your managerial skills to a laser beam. Each one of these items is direct and to the point. Apply each of these items to your own management style to help evaluate how you can improve your leadership skills. Enjoy...

✓ Players Play, Managers Manage

If you're a manager, concentrate solely on getting the best out of others. Lead by example and always be professional. Act as a guide and mentor to your team, but always remember you can't do their job for them.

✓ Take the time to understand each individual on your team

You will not be able to motivate people unless you discover precisely what it is that makes them tick. Learn about each individual; learn their background; know who you're dealing with.

✓ See in others more than they see in themselves

Your job as a manager is to identify the potential in others and instill confidence into your staff. Then you need to make sure they fulfill it.

✓ Responsibility equals accountability equals ownership

If people set their own targets, rather than receive them from a manager, they are more driven to reach them. Let your staff be a part of building the success.

11 – Leadership Lessons

✓ Surround yourself with people that are better than you

When you recruit and assemble your staff and management team, look for those who will challenge you and come up with original ideas and methods.

✓ Show your team how much you care

People don't care how much you know until they know how much you care. To get people to work harder, you need to show them that you genuinely do want them as individuals to achieve their career success.

✓ Evaluate yourself before you evaluate others

Don't rush to shift the blame onto others for their own underperformance. Be honest with yourself about what you could have done better. It is possible that you as their manager have failed them. Don't be tempted to blame others for underperforming yourself.

✓ Learn how to handle success

It's easier to get to the top than stay there. Don't let the cancer of complacency bring you down. Look forward to your next achievement and keep the drive moving forward.

✓ Conviction goes a long way

Managing is too important to be a part-time pursuit. Be prepared to go the extra mile and you will be rewarded in proportion.

11 – Leadership Lessons

Exceptional leaders build solid cornerstones:

* **Productivity** ...gets the job done
* **Credibility** ...consistency
* **Information** ...knowledge is the lifeblood of leadership
* **Positioning** ...awareness of your place in the process

Characteristics that describe of a Good Leader:

- Integrity	- High Energy	- Team Player
- Articulate	- Positive	- Strong Worker
- Creative	- Competitive	- Hungry for Success
- Adaptable	- Flexible	- Relationship Builder
- Passionate	- Quick Study	- Good Self Image
- Prideful	- Willingness	- Dedicated to Excellence
- Honesty	- Ask Questions	- Self Reliant
- Initiative	- Intelligent	- Problem Solver
- Insightful	- Goal Setter	- Self Confidence

11 – Leadership Lessons

Characteristics that describe a Non Leader:

- Distrust	- Disorganized	- Unpredictable
- Laziness	- Egotistical	- Indecisiveness
- Passive	- Poor Judge	- Self Centered
- Inward	- Evasiveness	- Inability to Delegate

When do leaders take a stand?

* When the overwhelming evidence is in your favor.
* When principle or integrity are at stake.
* When the life of your business is on the line.

When do leaders forfeit?

* When they are wrong.
* When they are not prepared.
* When the decision has been already been irrevocably made.

Good Leaders Care for Themselves

People management begins with the management of our selves. A continued self-development is essential for personal growth. There are four areas to consider and should turn into habits. It takes 21 days of repetition to institute a new habit. Always remember that we become what we feed our minds and souls.

11 – Leadership Lessons

First is to develop a disciplined reading program. Make the time to read with consistency. Be sure that it's something that interests you. This category is very broad and doesn't have to be educational or motivational. It could be newspaper articles, magazine articles, fictional books etc.

Second, listen to audio tapes. Find something that motivates you or teaches you something. An opportunity for this would be while traveling in the car. What better way to capture some valuable time and put it to good use. You will be able to experience the author's emotions as the words are spoken.

Third, participate in continuing education. Keep current on new developments in your field of expertise. Meet people outside of your inner circle doing what you're trying to accomplish. It is very rewarding to be a part of a group actively and consciously trying to better themselves.

Fourth, take good care of your body. Your physical well-being is important and connected to every aspect of this book. Get sufficient exercise, control your weight and get your rest. Your body and mind will appreciate it!

11 – Leadership Lessons

Chapter 12

Management Performance

*"Leadership and learning are
indispensable to each other"*

– John F Kennedy

12 – Management Performance

Is your management staff performing up to par! Are you having problems with expressing exactly what your expectations are? Does your management team understand you? Well if you're frustrated with their performance, these are some skills you'll want to see in your own management staff.

✓ A good manager needs to be a good planner with goals that must be attained. To attain these goals, they need both an immediate plan for the short term and more importantly, an on-going plan for the long term.

✓ To be a good manager, you have to like people and be good at communicating. This is hard to fake. If you don't enjoy interacting with people, it will be hard to manage them well. Teach your employees what their tasks and responsibilities are and give them the chance to share their ideas on how to reach their goals in the most efficient way. Giving direction in a respectful way is the key to success.

✓ You must have a wide range of personal contacts within your organization. You need relationships, not necessarily personal friendships, with a fair number of people. This includes your own employees. You must

12 – Management Performance

encourage these people to tell you what's going on and give you feedback about what people are thinking about the company and your role in it.

✓ Develop your people to do their jobs better than you can. Transfer your skills to them. This is an exciting goal, but it can be threatening to a manager who worries that he's training his replacement. The goal is to train managers that can cultivate future managers for expansion and growth. Be sure that there's no shortage of jobs for good managers.

✓ Build morale. Give people the sense of the importance of what they're working on - the importance to the company and the importance to customers.

✓ Take on projects yourself. You need to do more than communicate. The last thing people want is a boss who just doles out stuff. From time to time, prove you can be hands-on by taking on one of the less attractive tasks and using it as an example of how your employees should meet challenges.

✓ Don't be indecisive. Spend the time and thought to make a solid decision the first time so that you don't revisit the same issue time after time. Indecisive leadership interferes not only with your execution but also with your motivation to make a decision in the first place. People hate indecisive leadership. However, that doesn't mean you have to decide everything the moment it comes to your attention, nor does it mean that you can't ever reconsider a decision.

✓ A manager must delegate tasks to his employees but he can't give away the ultimate responsibility. He builds a

12 – Management Performance

team with specific responsibilities and these staff members take ownership; they must care about the final results of their tasks. Communication is important and when the tasks are completed, conversation and discussion regarding the outcome should follow.

✓ Motivate employees through acknowledgment and appreciation. Employees want to be respected. Create a reward system to encourage your employees to give their best. This could be as simple as a certificate of achievement presented at a meeting.

✓ Let people know whom to please. Maybe it's you, maybe it's your boss, and maybe it's somebody who works for you. Have self-confidence; believe in yourself and your capabilities. Don't worry when something fails and optimistic when considering your next plans.

✓ Have patience and demonstrate flexibility with their team. Allow employees to give their opinion as to how work will be successfully completed. Flexibility means that there is a possibility of compromise. Don't take the attitude that you are the boss and only you know the right decisions. Give your employees sufficient time to complete their work. Patience is a key to success!

✓ Good managers are good teachers and they teach every day. There always teaching the staff how to improve. This process never ends.

✓ Leading by example and follow through are traits of highly successful professionals. Management will judge your attitude by your behavior and not just your words.

12 – Management Performance

✓ When managing sales people, the best results generally come if you allow sales people to work to their strengths; in a way that is natural to them.

...and finally,

✓ Be a consistent goal setter and encourage your staff to maintain the five characteristics of proper goal setting; specific, measurable, attainable, relevant & time-bound.

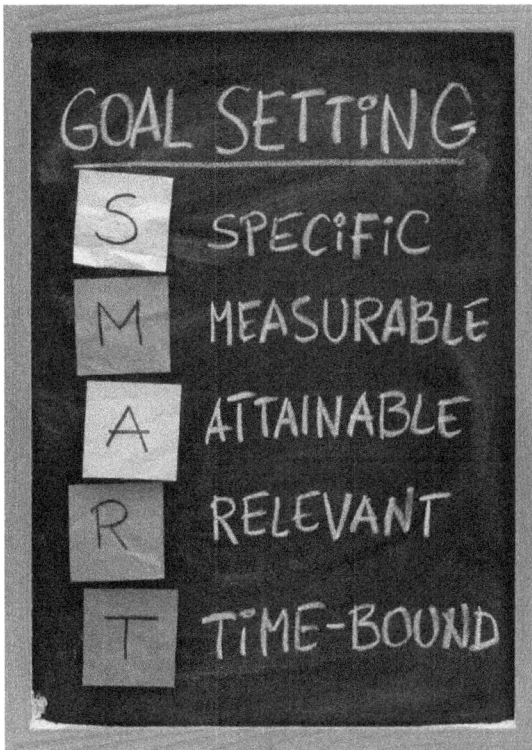

12 – Management Performance

Examples of some Do's and Don'ts for establishing leadership qualities:

Do: Pitch in and Solve Problems
Don't: Complain or Criticize

Example: You're really frustrated with the response time of another department. Instead of complaining about it, you can pitch in and help improve their deficiencies. Don't be surprised if everyone notices the improvement including your boss.

Do: Hands-On-Training
Don't: Lecture

Example: You're responsible for training a new employee. You can lecture him about the processes or you can involve your new coworker and walk through it together with real life examples and demonstrations.

Do: Serve as a Role Model
Don't: Boast About Your Success

Example: If you are a mentor, don't just meet with your partner; let him observe you on the job. Not only will he learn more, but will view you as a leader and have a greater respect for you and the company.

12 – Management Performance

Do: Just Do It!
Don't: Just Volunteer

Example: Don't just volunteer to write a report or create a new sales idea. Without even asking permission, just do it. Your boss will be impressed that you've identified the need and took the initiate without being asked. Being motivated and self-directed are traits of successful professionals.

Do: Act like a Manager
Don't: Wait for a Title

Example: Avoid gossip and prove that you are part of the solution rather than part of the problem. In a competitive environment, candidates need to back up their claims and the only way to earn a raise or promotion is through results.

Becoming a successful manager is not an easy task. It's not just a matter of making the right decisions for your company. You must also be a good leader, which means that you need to understand how to best handle various problems. Knowledge is necessary, but having a good vision of the future of your company and having the ability to create a good working team is more important. The store is a reflection of the person in charge. It takes on a personality representing the character of the manager or owner.

12 – Management Performance

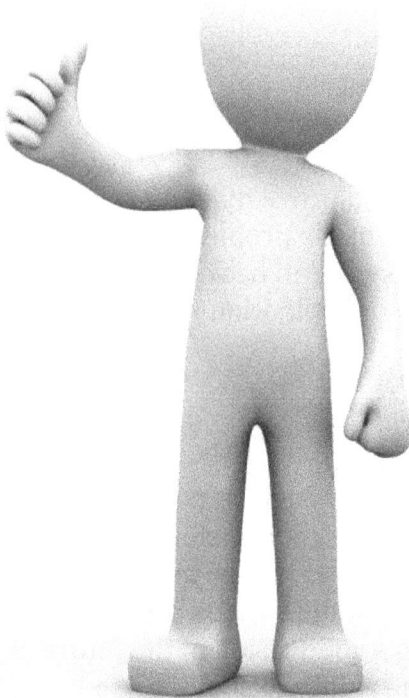

Chapter 13

End of the Month *PUSH!*

*"In the confrontation between the stream
and the rock, the stream always wins -
not through strength but by perseverance."*

– H. Jackson Brown

13 – End of the Month *PUSH!*

The traditional approach to Sales Management is to focus on the end of month figures, yet a more effective method is to guide the sales team through the month to ensure a successful end result. You must implement effective strategies to encourage your team and keep them focused, even when targets seem out of reach.

It is crucial you know how to motivate your sales team without being too forceful. It is your job as a sales manager to ensure everybody is working their hardest towards a common goal - end of month targets. This is not always easy. What do you do if you find yourself struggling mid-month to keep up with your monthly sales goal? Here are some ideas you can put into place to help make a struggling month.

12 Ideas to Help Make the Month

1. Hold a "Pep Rally" sales meeting to excite your troops to go into battle on the sales battlefield. Enlist their support to create a synergy among the staff.

2. Use existing floor traffic to increase volume of sales.

    a. Staff practicing the "Add-On" & "Suggestive Selling" techniques *[challenge staff to sell an additional 3 items per customer]*

    b. Consistently using the "Up-Selling" technique when applicable *[show features & benefits of higher quality items]*

13 – End of the Month *PUSH*!

3. Create some "In Store" promotions, increasing interest in more products per customer.

4. Got any "On Hold" items? Call those customers for a speedy pick up.

5. Call all leads and invite them into the store to close the deal. Create urgency!

6. Finalize your prepaid sales like special orders, deposits, layaways, etc...

7. Network local clubs, associations, church groups, etc...

8. Create a contest for sales staff and set goals per sales person. Track results and show standings on a poster board for visual affirmation.

9. Initiate a contest between multiple store locations. Track results and encourage staff to compete throughout the competition.

10. Schedule your best full time sales staff to be on the floor during busiest peak selling times.

11. Every customer is approached and greeted to company policy and standards.

12. Network your customers to get more leads and potential sales. *[Invite them back into your store before the monthly promotions end)*

How many more ideas can you list to help make the month?

13 – End of the Month *PUSH!*

Chapter 14

15 RED HOT Ways to be More Profitable!

"There are no great limits to growth because there are no limits of human intelligence, imagination, and wonder"

– Ronald Reagan

14 – 15 RED HOT Ways to be More Profitable

The purpose of a business is to make a profit while satisfying customers. There are only a few ways to increase the operating profit of your business; A: increase sales price, B: increase sales volume, C: reduce cost and D: staff training. Profitability is a great concern for businesses especially in today's economy. Consider the samples listed below to get your business moving into the right direction.

1. Increase your pricing on accessories 10% - 15% today. Some items may not fit these criteria and other items could be increased at a greater percentage. Quality, service and selection are more important than price as a profit driver.

2. Teach staff to sell more top line product (items with greater profit, private label, etc...).

3. Create & initiate events and clinics at your store to create more community awareness and possible press opportunities. Get involved with your local school and community organizations.

4. Write a "Press Release" for the newspaper. Get attention through your local papers or magazines to help promote events and clinics.

14 – 15 RED HOT Ways to be More Profitable

5. Focus staff on $ per transactions. Analyze the register sales journal and look for single item transactions. A contest could be a great incentive.

6. Training session on sales techniques (asking the "right" questions during the sale, closing techniques etc...).

7. Create a contest for the staff – always chart their success on a board in the back room and reward the winners in view of the other staff.

8. Focus on your part time staff to be as knowledgeable and as sharp as your full time staff.

9. Have a greater awareness to individual sales goals and forecast for the store. The staff needs to know the bench marks to achieve success.

10. Manage your payroll like a hawk (clocking in/out times, eliminating over coverage when possible, etc...).

11. Monitor utilities usage. Set guidelines for everybody to follow (electric, air conditioning, heater, water, building insulation, etc...).

12. Analyze the cost of store use items and trim the fat where possible. Buy in bulk and monitor supplies.

13. Reduce or eliminate unnecessary reoccurring expenses like subscriptions, etc... Some task can be done by your existing staff like window cleanings, janitorial services, subscriptions, etc...

14. Follow your check approval procedures – less bad debts can be a huge savings to the bottom line profits.

15. Create a special promotion on high profit items needing to be pushed, anything from unusual items or your favorite impulse items.

Why stop at 15!!!

---

16. Create an accessories item list to assist with larger item sales. It never hurts to have the appropriate add-ons at your fingertips and for the customer to use. Everything seems more believable in print!

17. Create a gift guide promotional flyer highlighting items under $10, $20 & $50. This is perfect for impulse shopper.

18. Be sure that your staff has business cards and uses them any chance they can. This is the best economical form of advertising around.

19. Never leave burned out light bulbs in the lighting fixture. This will only result in burning out the ballast while still consuming energy. Either replace bulbs or remove them from the fixture. Be sure not to sacrifice the light needed to display your product.

20. Eliminate out of stock product. Be sure to keep sufficient quantities (and sizes) of your staple product plus an assortment of unique or impulse items to sell to your customers. The idea is to never lose a customer. Chances are they are going to walk directly to your competitor making it hard to get them back.

21. Increase product expertise, sales resources and selling activity by inviting suppliers to provide one of their own merchandising/sales personnel to work in your store for an agreed period of time. Even if only for one day, the benefits could be great. Consider involving numerous suppliers to increase the exposure for your store and staff.

22. Slow moving products with large stock levels can be bundled with a fast moving item, which can be offered together at an attractive price. This extends value to the customer, and helps to reduce the stock level of the slow-moving items.

23. Virtual Products Program – a way to sell your merchandise without having to stock it. The purchased product is treated as a special order and payment or a deposit is made prior to ordering the merchandise. A display of catalogs can be setup to facilitate a breadth of product to be offered.

How many more ideas can you list of how you can help be more profitable?

Chapter 15

Employee Effectiveness

*"Everything depends upon execution;
having just a vision is no solution."*

- Stephen Sondheim

15 – Employee Effectiveness

Great leaders must develop evaluation skill to keep the ship sailing smoothly, kind of like trimming the sails, making adjustments to get all you can out of an associate. You need to know the capabilities of your staff. By evaluating the effectiveness of your associates you will be able to recognize a lack of aptitude or discover strengths that you didn't know existed.

The employee evaluation is a great opportunity to reward a good employee or can be used as a tool to identify problems needing attention or associates that need to be replaced. This process should be done bi-annually or at least annually. Use the Employee Evaluation Form (supplement 1) to find out how each staff member is executing the expectations set forth by their superiors. It will show certain areas that need improvement and will document the salespersons level of expertise and should be kept in their HR file. If you have an employee that is showing signs of discontent or a need for quick improvement, this tool is a good way to identify and document the results before replacement is a consideration.

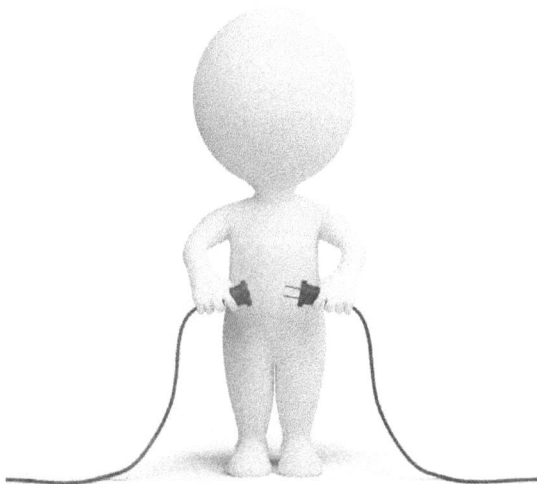

15 – Employee Effectiveness

Performance appraisal:

1. Goals:

    a. Reward good performance

    b. Motivate to improve performance

    c. Determine current goals

    d. Determine salary/incentive/benefits

2. Standards:

    a. Consistent

    b. Fair

    c. Prompt

    d. Objective

    e. Relevant

    f. Documented

Through this process you may be able to uncover alternatives to motivate an associate but keep in mind that a more capable candidate may be the best option.

Here's what you want to find out:

• How consistent is your sales staff with the operational procedures of your company and their ability to maintain motivation for themselves and others around them?

15 – Employee Effectiveness

* What is their ability to lead by example (sales stats, leads collected, attitude, selling techniques)?

* Are they able to develop a network within the community?

* What are their organizational qualities like and ability to work well with others and plan ahead?

* How well do they communicate with others and superiors?

* Are their merchandising skills up to par?

* How is their performance of executing sales promotions?

Asking the right specific questions can tell you volumes of information that can help you determine each of your associates weaknesses and assets. With the right coaching you will be able to correct any misguiding or improper attitudes. Failure to act on a solution would only perpetuate bad habits and poor performance. The path of least resistance is not necessarily the best course of action to follow. Procrastination is a major obstacle that will impede positive forward motion.

Causes for procrastination:

1. Lack of knowledge or training to do the task.
2. Past mistakes in similar endeavors.
3. The fear of failure immobilizes many.
4. A lack of self-confidence or poor self-esteem.
5. Dislike for the task causing a lack of enthusiasm.
6. A lack of discipline.

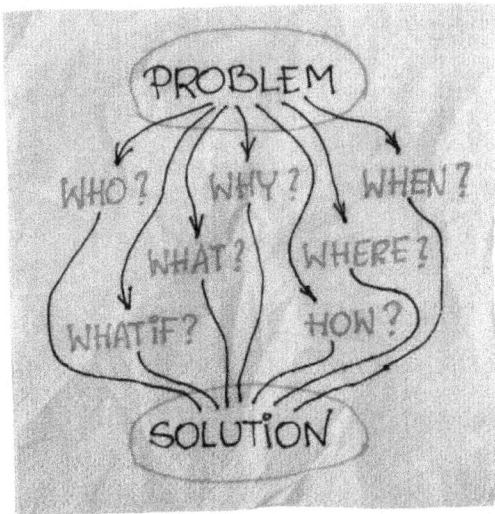

Major areas for complaint:

1. Hire/fire practices
2. Pay inconsistencies

3. Implied contract

4. Working conditions

5. Promotion / advancement

6. Layoff

7. Benefits

Motivating factors:

1. Tangible motivators:

    a. Money

    b. Fringe benefits

    c. Profit opportunity

    d. Office surroundings

    e. Awards and prizes

2. Intangible motivators:

    a. Sense of belonging

    b. Personal growth – Training

    c. Promotion opportunity

    d. Recognition and appreciation

    e. Differentiation

    f. Security

    g. Job challenge

    h. Promises kept

15 – Employee Effectiveness

Understanding criticism and its benefits:

Criticism opens you up to new perspectives and new ideas you may not have considered. Whenever someone challenges you, they help expand your thinking. It's not easy to take an honest look at yourself and your weaknesses, but you can only grow if you're willing to try. There are many benefits to be realized like personal growth, emotional health, improved relationships & self-confidence.

When someone criticizes you, it shines a light on your own insecurities. It is cruel to criticize someone in front of another. You must direct the criticism at "what's" wrong and not "who's" wrong. The following filters can be used when giving criticism:

1. Can it be changed?
2. Is it the right time?
3. Would affirmation help?
4. Is it specific?
5. Have you expressed confidence in their ability to change?

The best way to deal with criticism is to assume that all criticism is friendly. You should strive to recognize the grain of truth in each criticism.

If you've received 100 words of praise and one criticism, which one would you remember?

Questions you should ask your management team:
(You may be surprised at the answers you get!)

1. What do you perceive your job description to be?

2. What is your perception of duties you were hired to perform?

3. If you were to add a task to your list of duties that would help you be more successful, what would it be?

4. What obstacles are preventing you from achieving your goals?

5. If you could do anything you wanted in life, what would you be doing now?

6. What do you consider is your special gift that makes you unique?

Chapter 16

Staffing!
How to Hire the Right Person

"If you pick the right people and give them the opportunity to spread their wings: you almost don't have to manage them"

— Jack Welch

16 – Staffing!

How to Hire the Right Person

Hiring the right employee is a gamble and a challenging process. Hiring the wrong employee is expensive, costly to your work environment, and time consuming. Hiring the right employee, on the other hand, pays you back in employee productivity, a successful employment relationship, and a positive impact on your total work environment. Hiring the right employee enhances your work culture and pays you back a thousand times over in high employee morale, positive forward thinking planning, and accomplishing challenging goals. This is not a comprehensive guide to hiring a new employee, but rather some key steps to hiring the right employee.

16 – Staffing!

Step 1: Defining the Job

The job description will assist you in planning your recruiting strategy for hiring the right employee. Collect information about the duties, necessary skills, expectations, work environment and the reporting relationship within the company. These elements should clearly identify and spell out the responsibilities of a specific job. The best job descriptions do not limit employees, but rather, cause them to stretch their experience, grow their skills, and develop their ability to contribute within their organization. The following is a list items to consider including:

→ Qualifications
→ Responsibilities
→ Term
→ Necessary skills
→ Expectations
→ Accountability
→ Support

Step 2: Review Your Applicants

Screen all applicants against this list of qualifications, skills, experience, and characteristics. You'll want to spend most of your time with your most qualified candidates when hiring a new employee. Eliminate resumes with poor work histories or not enough length of time per position. Some resumes may not fit the characteristics that you're looking for. Example: previous sales experience, computer skills, specific industry background, serious drops in salary, grammar/spelling, availability, etc... Use the "Applicant Phone Screening Form" (supplement 11) to organize your candidates as you call them to set an appointment. The most important reason to prescreen candidates when hiring an employee is to save the interviewer from wasting time. While a candidate may look good on paper, a prescreening interview will tell you if their qualifications are truly a fit with your job. Additionally, in a prescreening interview, you can determine whether their salary expectations are congruent with your job. A skilled telephone interviewer will also obtain evidence about whether the candidate may fit within your culture - or not. Only candidates that meet all of your requirements should be considered.

Step 3: Candidate Selection

Let your candidate know that the interview process can take anywhere from 30 minutes to an hour. They will need to fill out some papers before the actual interview begins. Some interviews may take longer than others depending on how well the interview is going. Some may be very short depending on how good or bad your first impression is. Don't hesitate to move on to your next candidate as soon as you're sure the current applicant is not appropriate for the position.

Finding Candidates: *Which ones are appropriate for your business?*

➜ Your company website

➜ Your personal network

➜ Current and former employees

➜ Craigslist

➜ Career websites: LinkedIn and other specific business sites

16 – Staffing!

→ Social media sites: Facebook, Twitter, Google+, etc.

→ Industry associations

→ Career centers at schools/colleges/universities

→ Signs posted in window

→ Newspaper help wanted ads

→ Unemployment office

Five traits you want to see in your dream candidate:

✓ **Dedication;**
Ability to see their work through to completion.

✓ **Responsibility;**
Good character is the foundation to making proper choices.

✓ **Education;**
Recognizes and creates opportunities to take control.

✓ **Attitude;**
Demonstrates initiative and resourcefulness to get things done.

✓ **Motivation;**
Positive reinforcement affecting themselves and everyone around them.

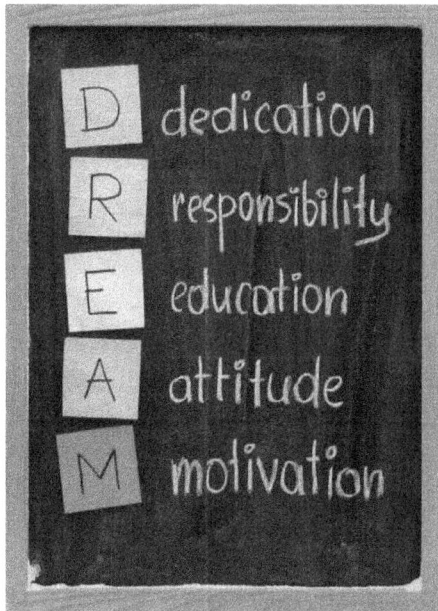

D dedication
R responsibility
E education
A attitude
M motivation

16 – Staffing!

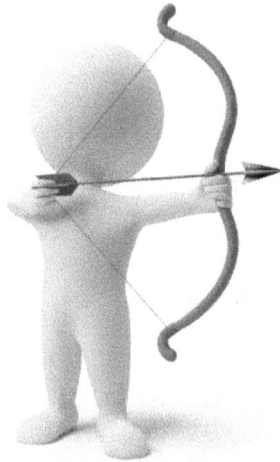

Step 4: The Interview Process:

A structured sequence to each interview is important for continuity. Have the candidate fill out the application first before the interview begins. Punctuality is important for your candidate as well as the interviewer. A first impression is had on both sides of the fence and sets a precedent going forward. You'll want to be thorough while asking your questions. Ask open-ended questions. Avoid questions that can be answered with a simple yes or no, and questions that have an obvious right answer. You want open ended, thought provoking questions that begin with what, when, where, how or why. The answers can be very revealing. A list of possible questions can be found in the supplemental section titled "Interview Questions for New Applicants" (supplement 12). This will enable you to match their experience to your needs as a candidate for the position. Being organized is crucial during the interview process. Use the "Personnel Interview Analysis Form" (supplement 13) to help score each applicant on the following 10 key areas:

16 – Staffing!

1. Product Knowledge

2. Depth of Sales / Retail Experience

3. Ability to Communicate

4. Ability to Work with Others

5. Interest in Position & Company

6. Motivation & Drive

7. Appearance (in relation to job)

8. Personality (in relation to job)

9. Overall Demeanor / Confidence

10. Employment History

16 – Staffing!

Be sure to leave time at the end of the interview for questions. A two way communication can be insightful. When candidates ask questions, you get to see how they think and find out what's important to them. The best candidates will ask you meaningful questions about the job. Of course, they will also ask about salaries and benefits.

Step 5: Following Up:

Effective background checks are one of the most important steps when hiring an employee. You need to verify that all of the presented credentials, skills, and experience are actually possessed by your candidate. The background checks must include work references, especially former supervisors, educational credentials, employment references and actual jobs held, and criminal history. Other background checks when hiring an employee, such as credit history, must be specifically related to the job for which you are hiring an employee.

A phone call to the candidate is the first step after you have decided that he or she is not the most qualified for your open position. During the call, you thank them for their application and interview time. State clearly that you have determined that you have other candidates who are more qualified for the position. Then, follow-up your call with the official letter providing the same information. This contact should occur as soon as you know the candidate is not the person you want to hire. Don't leave your candidates wondering for weeks on end if they are not the person who will be selected for the job. A sample rejection letter can be found in the supplemental section (supplement 15).

A standard applicant rejection letter can be used for the resumes and applications you receive from applicants who are

16 – Staffing!

less qualified than those you decide to interview. A sample can be found in the supplemental section (supplement 14). Since many of these applications arrive in email, response via email is acceptable.

A rejection letter may momentarily make the candidate sad, but it's better for both the employer and the candidate to share official notification. Plus, in an effective rejection letter, you can indicate whether you have an ongoing interest despite the fact that you had a more qualified candidate that you hired for this job.

Step 6: Extending a Job Offer:

Congratulations on finding the right person for the job! It's not an easy task as you can see, but the rewards for all of your hard work are just beginning. This phone call should be an easy one. Be sure to confirm the details of which they were hired and get a verbal commitment. Setting expectations should begin at the moment the new associate is hired. This doesn't have to be elaborate but rather concise and to the point. A simple statement will lay the foundation for you to establish a loyal and winning attitude.

A sample job offer letter that will confirm your verbal agreements can be found in the supplemental section (supplement 16). Keep in mind that the acceptance of the position is only tentative until the offer letter and the confidentiality agreement (if you use one) are signed.

Can I Afford Another Employee?

The decision to hire more staff is a tough one. You want enough people to handle the workload and service your growing customer base. At the same time, however, you don't want to hire too many people and pay salaries to idle hands.

Growing the business can be very exciting. There's a justifiable fear for the unknown. Will the increase of personnel result in enough additional sales to cover my cost? Don't discount the intangibles when considering expansion of staff members. The synergy and excitement that could be created can be invaluable.

Ask yourself these questions before weighing the pros and cons of adding new staff members to your team. If you answer "yes" to the majority of these questions, adding an employee might benefit your company:

- Are your current employees unable to finish their work and are you having to extend deadlines for your employees? *(When everything is done on time or early, you may have too many employees.)*

- Is the overall quality of work in your company slipping?

- Is there a lot of frustration and stress about getting work done?

- Do you have additional work or new clients coming in?

16 – Staffing!

* Are your employees complaining about long hours and demanding work conditions.

* Have you not had the time to review your increasing profit, realizing you have plenty of money to hire more help to keep up with demand?

* Have your overtime costs have increased?

* Are your employees able to take lunches, breaks, and vacations?

* Have you been unable to improve technology or processes because employees don't have the time to focus on developing more efficient methods?

* Has sales revenue been going above and beyond payroll costs?

* Is it easy for you to justify how a new employee would improve your bottom line because the employee would complete work that brings in more profit?

When is the right time to expand staff? I've listed some pros and cons for consideration. A worksheet is listed below with a formula to help some numbers behind your decision.

16 – Staffing!

Here are some things to consider when hiring a new associate:

Pros:

- Increase your sales & serve more customers.
- Redistribute work load to help you concentrate on the work you do best.
- Better salesmanship & balance your weaknesses.
- Demonstrates to the existing staff the seriousness of being effective.
- Fresh new ideas added to the mix & potential future growth.
- Excitement for crew to work with new personnel and help train.
- Existing staff's skills will benefit from training new staff members.

16 – Staffing!

Cons:

* Cost of training (payroll, supplies, extended time needed etc...)
* Time consuming for supervisor and subordinates that help train and manage.
* Lost time for networking in the community.
* Potential loss of customers & continuity of existing contacts.

Item Description   Amount

A.   Current monthly profit $_____

B.   Est. increased monthly income $_____

C.   **Subtotal:** Add "A" and "B" $_____

D.   Expected monthly salary/wages $_____

E.   Estimated monthly taxes/benefits $_____

F.   Estimated other monthly costs $_____

G.   **Subtotal:** Add "D", "E" and "F" $_____

   TOTAL: Subtract "G" from "C"   **$_____**

16 – Staffing!

FYI - *While you're considering how much you can afford for a new employee, remember to also budget for payroll taxes and benefits. As a rule of thumb, budget 15-30% of their salary for additional expenses. You'll also want to check out any current tax incentives through government programs or local job growth incentives.*

Chapter 17

Staff Meeting Guidelines

*"I hear and I forget, I solve and I remember,
I do and I understand"*

— Confucius

17 – Staff Meeting Guidelines

This is an opportunity to zap your staff. There should be a minimum of two meetings per month. Each meeting should focus on sales training and once a month there should be a focus on product knowledge. Your meetings should be positive and energizing to attend.

General Guidelines for a Productive Meeting

Before the Meeting:

- Choose a time and location that will be convenient for everyone involved.

- Make sure all individuals know the time and location well in advance. A second reminder or a strategic phone call may be in order to stress the seriousness of being on time, if not a little bit early.

- Be well prepared. Do your homework on the issues to be discussed. Clearly define the purpose and goals of the meeting.

17 – Staff Meeting Guidelines

- Prepare a written agenda to distribute to your staff at the meeting. It should include the following; review agenda, review data reports and statistics, training topics and discussions, review goals and expectations, set next meeting.

- Assign times for each agenda item. Make sure the meeting's goals are realistic for the time allotted. In general, it's best to limit meetings to two hours.

Expectations:

- The staff should arrive 15 minutes prior to the start time of the meeting to ensure a prompt start. This must be clearly communicated to everyone so that the meeting is able to start on time and without any distractions from late arrivers.

- Each participant should be alert and attentive throughout the entire meeting.

- Each participant should be helpful and positive with an engaging attitude.

- The facilitator helps group members stay focused and productive. An effective facilitator, who keeps participants on track, ensures the accomplishment of expected, desired results from the meeting.

17 – Staff Meeting Guidelines

Order of Events:

- Begin the meeting on time with a review of your agenda.

- Continue with the data reports and statistics. Documentation that will help you can include reports like Sales Month-to-Date, Percent to Forecast, Items Per Transaction, Profitability Margin, Microsoft® PowerPoint slides that illustrate key discussion points and follow-up from earlier or related meetings.

- Specific training: Sales strategies or Product knowledge. Include an activity that engages the staff.

- Review group goals with expectations. Possibly initiate a contest to help focus your crew on a specific target.

Visual Aids & Staff Involvement:

- The presenter should have a writing board to work from (dry erase or marker board). Your staff needs to see certain elements of the information to be able to fully digest the information and peek their interest.

- Try to include something colorful in your demonstrations. Color adds a new dimension to keep the mind interested.

- Ask questions to get your staff's input. This will help your staff to feel ownership and pride in the store and ultimately their buy in. A good technique is to ask questions that will lead your staff in the direction you want them to go.

17 – Staff Meeting Guidelines

- Have a demonstration planned using your staff and props. This can be in the form of storytelling or acting out a situation.

- Role Plays are excellent to solidify your training methods. Discuss real life scenarios and barriers to success that team members may experience as they try to accomplish the items that will produce the required results.

- Involve each participant in actions. Every work group has various personalities that show up for meetings; Quiet co-workers vs. staff who try to dominate every platform. Whether facilitating or attending the meeting, you need to involve each attendee. This ensures that each participant is invested in the topic of the meeting.

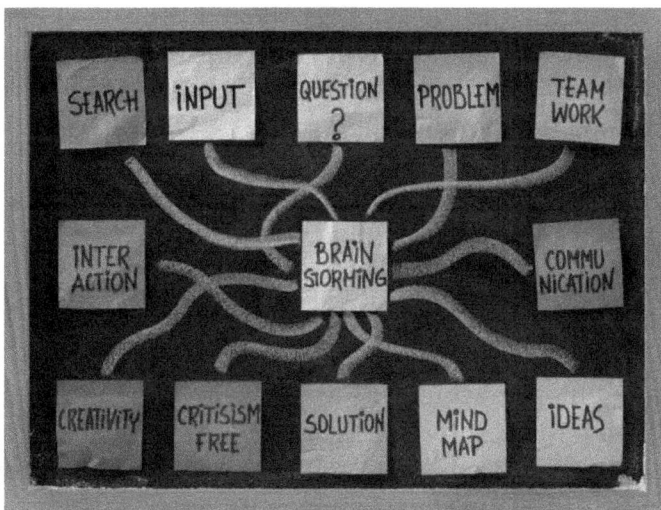

www.SolutionsForSelling.com

After the Meeting:

- Create an effective meeting follow-up plan. During the meeting, make a follow-up plan with action items. Effective plans include:

    A. The specific action item
    B. The name of the person who committed to owning the accomplishment of the action item
    C. The due date of the action item
    D. An agreement about what constitutes completion of the action item

- Publish your meeting minutes and action plan within 24 hours. People will most effectively contribute to results if they get started on action items right away. They still have a fresh memory of the meeting, the discussion and the rationale for the chosen direction. They remain enthusiastic and ready to get started. A delay in the distribution of minutes will hurt your results since most people wait for the minutes to arrive before they begin to tackle their commitments.

- Your actions and planning before and during the meeting play a big role in helping you achieve expected, positive, and constructive outcomes. Your actions following the meeting are just as crucial.

Great results are achievable and predictable from well-planned and implemented meetings. Follow these recommendations to ensure that meeting attendees achieve expected, positive, and constructive outcomes from your meetings.

Chapter 18

Marketing Strategies for Today's Business

"Management is efficiency in climbing the ladder of success; leadership determines whether the ladder is leaning against the right wall."

— Stephen R. Covey

18 – Marketing Strategies for Today's Business

What you need to do is open up your yellow pages and pick out a local marketing company to implement a complicated, labor intensive and very expensive marketing campaign!

... Say Whaaaat?

Well, not these days, think again. First of all, the days of opening up a big yellow book to find out business information is becoming a thing of the past. Technology is rapidly changing the way we are doing business so the way we market our business also needs to be changed to fit an ever developing consumer.

To understand how to approach a marketing plan for your business, it may be helpful to understand today's definition of marketing.

Marketing:

Creating an experience that engages your customer and differentiates you from your competition, developing relationships with your customers - getting people to come back again and again.

1. Define Your Brand and Discover Your Uniqueness

Develop a statement representing who you are and what you offer. Think of creating an elevator speech for someone that only has a matter of seconds to find out if you fit their needs. This should be a max of three sentences and preferably one! Items to consider should include any specific skills, potential customers, competition, emotional benefits like image and feeling. Surveys or questionnaires can gather details from your existing customer base. Also try to poll potential customers if possible by using an acquired database list of shoppers in your geographical area. If you are successful in discovering your uniqueness, customers will want what you have and won't be able to get it anywhere else.

2. Develop a Strategy to *Run with the Big Dogs!*

Before you decide on any form of advertising, you must adopt and commit to a marketing strategy. All tactical decisions should be filtered through your strategy to see if they make sense or support the overall marketing strategy. You will need to define your mission and pinpoint your target audience. Ask yourself questions like "What makes them happy?" and "What do they want?" Know your customers and figure out how to make the connection. Be sure not to make the common mistake of assuming to be all things to all people.

The concept of a marketing strategy may seem foreign or out of reach, but it's really little more than determining and narrowly defining your ideal client and creating a way to communicate a key point of differentiation. Keep in mind that simply saying you offer great service isn't a differentiator, it's an expectation.

18 – Marketing Strategies for Today's Business

In today's business world, there are many methods of advertising to reach your audience. Traditional methods like print (newspaper, magazines, journals, direct mail, etc...) or radio/TV aren't the only choices anymore. The ROI (return on investment) should be monitored very closely if you want to continue these methods of marketing since technology has given the business owner many more affordable means to reach your targeted audience.

The Social Media landscape is made up of many entities like LinkedIn, Twitter, Facebook, blogging, RSS feeds, YouTube, etc... These are just a few of the high profile components, when put together can be a very powerful marketing machine. These components and others are briefly described in the following sections.

3. Create a Web Presence, not just a website

It's simply not enough to have a website and think you're really participating online. The majority of purchase decisions made today involved some amount of research online.

Your website can be a great ambassador or even your best consistent salesmen working 24/7/365! An investment of time is well spent to develop a top notch website to promote your business.

Web sites tend to be written by technical people. Thus lots of websites are more like technical manuals instead of being consumer friendly. Make sure you are using a web designer that understands marketing and selling. Most of all make sure they understand people. Every business relies on connecting with people - particularly online, where it is a bit harder to make a personal connection and build loyalty.

Basic Principles for a successful website

✓ **Inviting:** Your website is an extension of your physical storefront. It too should be welcoming. Graphic images, such as buttons or tabs, should be clearly labeled and easy to read. Your web graphic designer should select the colors, backgrounds, textures, and special effects on your web graphics very carefully.

✓ **Informational & Educational:** A clear defined message of who you are and what you do is important to establish an easy report with your prospective customers. Positioning your business as the authority in its field is a valuable resource and will also give your customers a reason to visit. Being considered part of the establishment will eliminate many objections before they arise. The design should exhibit a company's values and culture; while at the same time educate the viewer.

✓ **Promotional** *(sales & events):* Consider your site to be a home base for your public to find out what your current promotions are. A list of upcoming events will keep your customers informed and increase their participation.

Functionality for a successful website

✓ **Ease of Navigation:** Simplicity is the key. If your customers get confused or if it takes any considerable energy they are likely to bounce off your site and onto another. The rules of engagement are simple ...Simplicity.

✓ **Collection of Information:** Opportunity to capture data about the individuals that visit your site and what attracts them to each section. You should follow the statistics of how long they visit and where they are from.

✓ **Lead Generator:** Businesses that offer services and higher end products need a steady stream of sales leads to keep the business going and growing. Leads are critical for the success of any selling organization. Your website is the perfect opportunity to generate excitement for your product and capture qualified leads. It makes sense to create a powerful online source of lead generation for your organization.

✓ **Consistent Message:** Customers respond to honesty and trustworthiness. Your website provides an opportunity to establish your brand with integrity. The consistency makes it believable.

Note: e-commerce websites will have many more levels of complexity to achieve capturing sales without a store front.

"Must Have's" for a successful website

✓ **SEO (search engine optimization):** Today's business must be easily engaged online, easily communicated with online and easily found by online search engines like Google, Yahoo & MSN. This requires a major focus on SEO and social media participation. You need to design your website with SEO in mind. A good web designer will incorporate basic SEO into a site as they build it. Not that optimization is more important than web design; however a lack of design will also lead to loosing traffic, known as your bounce rate. SEO will get a site noticed. It will get visitors. Keeping those visitors requires a little extra though. Both Web design and SEO are extremely important.

Adding the right content and elements so the search engines' spiders (the bot that searches your page) can index and scroll your pages easily. Search engines also look at the number of sites that link to your page. The more sites that link to your page, the better your ranking will be.

4. Adopt a Social Media Model:

Like various clubs or associations, LinkedIn, Facebook, Twitter and blog communities are like separate paces to hang out. Each social media tool offers distinctly different atmospheres and amenities. Carefully consider your purpose and your willingness to get and stay involved.

Marketers today must commit to producing content much like a publisher might. Prospects expect to search and find large amounts of useful information. Consistent production of content that builds awareness and trust, such as client success stories and testimonials, or content that educates, such as blog posts, e-books and online seminars is a major component of the new marketing system.

The model you choose will help you establish a consistency with your voice. It should exemplify a consistent reliable experience.

Achievable goals through Social Media:

- Be found by those looking for you
- Be seen as an expert and a go-to resource
- Be available / accessible to customers and clients
- Attract new prospects
- Create brand awareness
- Maintain / improve your brand image
- Provide proactive customer service
- Gain strength with partnerships and strategic alliances

18 – Marketing Strategies for Today's Business

Social Sites:

i. **LinkedIn:** is a user-profile based database that houses users' professional background information, their contacts and their affiliated groups and associations. These comprise one's "network" and within a user's network, various interactions can occur through groups, events, or just periodic updates.

ii. **Twitter:** is a forum that consists of a running thread of 140 characters (or fewer) postings called "tweets." Through a very simple interface, users subscribe to (aka "follow") people of their choice with no obligation to follow anyone in particular. There's a huge advantage with this tool in that all significant news breaks on Twitter.

iii. **Facebook:** is more complex that LinkedIn, but is also far more conducive to ongoing conversations. Facebook's average user age is now over 40 for a couple of reasons. One, reconnecting with former classmates is free. Another reason is user-friendly photo sharing that is secure and without charge. Grandparents find they need to get on Facebook to see their grandkids' photos. Parents also sign up to keep in touch with their college or teenaged kids.

> ## *85% of qualified internet traffic is driven through search engines, however 75% of search users never scroll past the first page of results!*
>
> ** Source: WWW User Survey – Georgia Institute of Technology*

Blogs:

Blogs are distinctly structured websites that contain short, conversational-style articles (called "posts") each housed on a separate URL, that are date/time stamped and can be commented on by readers. Blogging provides benefits the other social media channels cannot.

Building readership and a blog following (usually called "subscriber base") requires producing interesting posts on a fairly regular basis. Readership are fueled by your reading of other blogs on related topics and commenting on them. These comments create links back to your blog and readership grows organically. Blog posts open new doors to effective search engine strength because they are written more casual than a technical piece (i.e., journal article). Popular sites you can post articles or blogs include: EzineArticles, GoArticles, WebProNews, ArticleDashboard, etc....

18 – Marketing Strategies for Today's Business

RSS (Really Simple Syndication):

RSS is a family of web feed formats used to publish frequently updated works—such as blog entries, news headlines, audio, and video in a standardized format. An RSS document is called a feed, web feed, or channel.

These documents are beneficial because they are works of content that are syndicated automatically. They benefit readers who want to subscribe to timely updates from favorite websites or to pull feeds from many sites into one place. RSS allows users to avoid manually inspecting all of the websites they are interested in, and instead subscribe to websites such that all new content is pushed onto their browsers when it becomes available

Press Release:

Online press releases are designed to help increase your online visibility, reach more people and increase search engine ranking. An online press release is similar to a traditional press release, but with added benefits like links to outside sources, images, audio, videos and more. Sites that provide online press release services include: PR Web, Vocus, Newswire Today, Fast Pitch, etc....

As with traditional press releases, there are several tips to consider when writing a press release:

• Remember whom, what, where, when, how and why. Give the details and stick to the facts.

• Make a strong start with an impactful headline and first paragraph. Grab the reader's attention.

18 – Marketing Strategies for Today's Business

- Use active voice and don't be afraid of assertive language.

- Don't be wordy. Less is more. Try to be as concise as possible.

- No jargon. Don't go over the readers' heads with language they may not understand. Plain, concise language is the key.

- Proofread. Read your release at least twice and have a friend check it out for typos and errors.

Keep in mind that once you create an online press release, you must also distribute it. Be sure to send it to appropriate contacts and, where appropriate, consider sending out the release via your social media channels like Twitter and Facebook.

Search Engine/Online Advertising:

There are numerous places to advertise online. Some of the most popular sites are Google AdWords, Yahoo! Search Marketing, Microsoft adCenter, etc... Many companies offer a pay-per-click (PPC) payment option allowing it to be very affordable. Pay per click is an Internet advertising model used to direct traffic to websites, where advertisers pay the publisher (typically a website owner) when the ad is clicked.

Video Media:

The most popular is YouTube, a video-sharing website on which users can upload, share, and view videos. One of the key features of YouTube is the ability of users to view its videos on web pages outside the site. Each YouTube video is accompanied by a piece of HTML, which can be used to embed it on a page outside the YouTube website. This functionality is often used to embed YouTube videos in social networking pages and blogs. Other popular video sites include Yahoo Video, Flickr, Photobucket, etc...

Do not look at the web in terms of SEO vs. Design, LinkedIn vs. Twitter, or Social Media vs. Online Advertising. Look at it in terms of a marketing medium and bring in everything. There is no more cost effective medium for marketing. Use it to its full potential to sell your business.

5. Develop a Marketing Calendar and stick to it!

Marketing momentum requires consistent work over the long term. The best way to handle this is to create a Yearly Marketing Calendar. A marketing calendar assists you in launching your marketing vehicles in a way that can drive you to your goal in a structured manner. This is a great planning device for organizing promotional campaigns and product launches, but it's also a great tool to schedule out the many projects that need to be completed on time.

A sample template (supplement 23) can be found in the back of this book. Remember this is only a template; you will want to adapt it to fit the needs of your business.

Supplements

The *"Supplemental Documents and Forms"* are listed below and a sample of each supplement can be viewed in this section. Every document, form or spreadsheet is fully editable and adaptable for your business when purchased with the separate publication titled **"Sales & Management Training Modules: Solutions For Selling"**. It can be purchased at **www.SolutionsForSelling.com**. These documents and forms will help simplify the daily operations of your business and aid with the concepts being taught in this book.

1	Employee Evaluation Form
2	Sales Team Agreement
3	Sales Binder
4	Own Your Zone! Daily "To Do" List
5	Networking Takes Flight!
6	Phone Challenge Worksheet
7	Sales Challenge Worksheet
8	Feedback Postcard
9	Lead Sheet (current – 7 days)
10	Lead Archive (older leads)
11	Applicant Phone Screening Form
12	Interview Questions for New Applicant
13	Interview Analysis Form

Supplement 1

Employee Evaluation

Date __/__/____

How do you rate yourself?

Score_____

* To be filled out by staff member and supervisor separately.
* Rate staff member or yourself from 1 (needs work) to 10 (ideal).
* Write a brief explanation for each question.

____ 1. Operational procedures?

____ 2. Sales motivation?

____ 3. Setting the example:

     A. Sales stats?

     B. Leads collected?

     C. Attitude / having fun?

     D. Demonstrating proper sales techniques?

____ 4. Networking with community?

____ 5. Organizational qualities?

____ 6. Works well with others?

____ 7. Planning ahead, having foresight?

____ 8. Communication with staff & superiors?

____ 9. Merchandising (floor stock & back room)?

____ 10. Execution of sales promotions?

Additional comments:

Supplement 2

Sales - Team Agreement

☐ Maintain and cultivate a positive attitude on the sales floor and around the entire staff at all times.

☐ Approach and welcome each customer shortly after they enter the store.

☐ Initiate conversation and ask the "right" questions to build relationships and gain customers confidence.

☐ Practice "Suggestive Selling" and "Best Buy" selling techniques with every customer. Have an "add-on" item ready for each section of your store or for every main item (anchor product) you sell.

☐ Actively cultivate leads and follow up within 48 hours. Document your findings in sales binder.

☐ Keep store neat, clean and organized (NCO). Maintain merchandised product to make a great impression for our customers.

☐ Attempt to never disappoint our customers, under promise &, over deliver.

☐ Always strive to achieve excellence in customer service.

Please check each box, sign and date to acknowledge you have read and understand each item listed above. Happy selling!

Staff _____ Date __/__/____

Print name _____

Manager _____ Date __/__/____

Print name _____

Supplement 3

Sales Binder

Each sales staff member should have a binder to track leads, prioritize goals, organize objectives and track their success. It should contain only official business and kept clean with a high level of professionalism. It's easy for this binder to get out of control so keep close tabs on the condition and accuracy of what's being logged. For instance, the current lead sheet should be filled out to company standards including the number of new leads expected per day. Each lead should have complete information for reference (name, phone #, description and follow up dated within 48 hours).

Items needed to purchase:
- ☑ 1 ½" three ring binder
- ☑ set of colored page dividers tabbed for labeling
- ☑ spiral bound notebook

Directions to create your staff sales binder:

1. Label binder front cover and side panel with associates name.
2. Label each colored divider with appropriate categories to fit your business needs. The following categories are meant to be a template for you to use to develop appropriate documents to fit the needs of your business allowing your sales staff to function at a high level of success.

   a. Current Leads (green tab) - Use the "Sales Lead Sheet" form (supplement 9). Have extras with holes punched ready for use.
   b. Old leads (blue tab) - Use the "Lead Tracker" form (supplement 10). Have extras with holes punched ready for use.
   c. Sales Reports (red tab) - issued from head office.
   d. Company Statistics (yellow tab) - issued from head office.
   e. Communication & Company Updates (purple tab) - emails, newsletters, etc.
   f. Contest / Promotions (white tab) - issued from management.

Own Your Zone!

Daily *"To Do"* List   Week of ___ / ___ / _____

- Assigned staff member is responsible for their zone.
- Closing manager is responsible for "End of Evening Duties". *(see below)*

Zone	**Staff Member**	Mon	Tues	Wed	Thru	Fri	Sat	Sun
Department A	_____	____	____	____	____	____	____	____
Department B	_____	____	____	____	____	____	____	____
Department C	_____	____	____	____	____	____	____	____
Department D	_____	____	____	____	____	____	____	____
Front Display	_____	____	____	____	____	____	____	____
Window Disp.	_____	____	____	____	____	____	____	____
Register Area	_____	____	____	____	____	____	____	____
Stock Room A	_____	____	____	____	____	____	____	____
Stock Room B	_____	____	____	____	____	____	____	____
Restroom	_____	____	____	____	____	____	____	____

"End of Evening Duties" for closing staff:

- Finalize point of sale registers & complete closing paperwork.
- Clean & clear counters of miscellaneous items.
- Return product on hold or left out from the days business.
- Create a "To Do List" to organize the next crew.
- Clean all glass with window cleaner.
- Vacuum floor.
- Set alarm and lock up.

Supplement 5

Networking Takes Flight!

Follow instructions below as you learn each step and write in the key word for each on the right side.

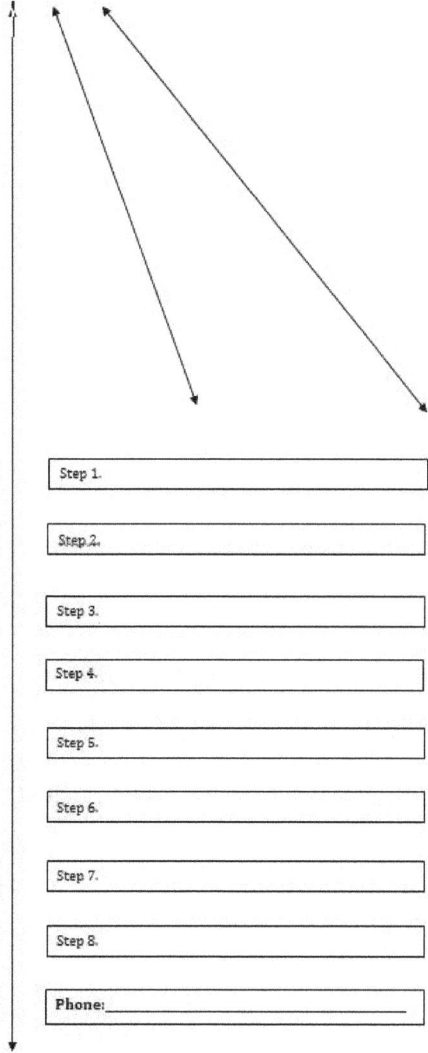

1. Fold in half, then unfold.	Step 1.
2. Fold the top right corner to center line.	Step 2.
3. Fold top right side to center line.	Step 3.
4. Repeat steps 2 & 3 for the left side.	Step 4.
5. Valley fold the model in half.	Step 5.
6. Fold the right wing down.	Step 6.
7. Fold the left wing down.	Step 7.
8. Label plane with your name & phone number.	Step 8.
Name:_____	Phone:_____

Supplement 6

Phone Challenge Worksheet

-- Mark a check when sales person retrieves the proper information.
-- If a competitor is mentioned, remove a check from the overall score!

Store #_____ Sales person_____ Date___/___/____

_____ 1. Greet customer properly using company script.

_____ 2. Establish a relationship through dialogue.

_____ 3. Find out who the item is for.

_____ 4. Make appropriate recommendation.

_____ 5. Add-on or up sale attempted.

_____ 6. Mention current sales promotion or promoted our products.

_____ 7. Identify a networking opportunity.

_____ 8. Get lead (name and phone number).

_____ 9. Invite customer to the store.

_____10. Was the sales person enthusiastic?

_____ **Score** (total # of checks received)

Evaluation chart:

9 or 10	Excellent
8	Good
7	Average
6 & lower	Needs improvement!

www.SolutionsForSelling.com

Supplement 7

Sales Challenge Worksheet

-- Mark a check when sales person retrieves the information.
-- If a competitor is mentioned, remove a check from the overall score!

Store #_____ Sales person_____ Date__/__/____

_____ 1. Greet customer properly (eye to eye contact).

_____ 2. Established a relationship through dialog.

_____ 3. Find out who the item is for.

_____ 4. Make appropriate recommendation.

_____ 5. Add-on or up sale attempted.

_____ 6. Mention current sales promotion or promoted our products.

_____ 7. Identify a networking opportunity.

_____ 8. Get lead (name and phone number).

_____ 9. Invite customer to return.

_____10. Was the sales person enthusiastic?

_____ **Score** (total # of checks received)

Evaluation chart:

10	Excellent
9	Good
8	Average
7 & lower	Needs improvement!

Supplement 8

Feedback Postcard

Thank you for shopping at our store.

We truly appreciate your feedback so that we can continue to improve. Please fill out and mail this postage paid survey or complete our survey online at www.simplesolutionsforselling.com

Rate each question on a scale from 1 to 10 with 10 being best.

_____ How would you rate your overall store experience?

_____ How would you rate your sales person (knowledge & personality)?

_____ Was the store organized so that you could find what you needed?

_____ Did the store cleanliness meet your expectations (restroom included)?

_____ How likely will you recommend us to your friends?

Additional comments: _____

Please fill out your information to receive our specials. We will respect your privacy.
Name _____ Email _____
Address _____ Phone _____
City _____ State _____ Zip _____

Thank you for shopping at our store.

We truly appreciate your feedback so that we can continue to improve. Please fill out and mail this postage paid survey or complete our survey online at www.simplesolutionsforselling.com

Rate each question on a scale from 1 to 10 with 10 being best.

_____ How would you rate your overall store experience?

_____ How would you rate your sales person (knowledge & personality)?

_____ Was the store organized so that you could find what you needed?

_____ Did the store cleanliness meet your expectations (restroom included)?

_____ How likely will you recommend us to your friends?

Additional comments: _____

Please fill out your information to receive our specials. We will respect your privacy.
Name _____ Email _____
Address _____ Phone _____
City _____ State _____ Zip _____

Thank you for shopping at our store.

We truly appreciate your feedback so that we can continue to improve. Please fill out and mail this postage paid survey or complete our survey online at www.simplesolutionsforselling.com

Rate each question on a scale from 1 to 10 with 10 being best.

_____ How would you rate your overall store experience?

_____ How would you rate your sales person (knowledge & personality)?

_____ Was the store organized so that you could find what you needed?

_____ Did the store cleanliness meet your expectations (restroom included)?

_____ How likely will you recommend us to your friends?

Additional comments: _____

Please fill out your information to receive our specials. We will respect your privacy.
Name _____ Email _____
Address _____ Phone _____
City _____ State _____ Zip _____

Thank you for shopping at our store.

We truly appreciate your feedback so that we can continue to improve. Please fill out and mail this postage paid survey or complete our survey online at www.simplesolutionsforselling.com

Rate each question on a scale from 1 to 10 with 10 being best.

_____ How would you rate your overall store experience?

_____ How would you rate your sales person (knowledge & personality)?

_____ Was the store organized so that you could find what you needed?

_____ Did the store cleanliness meet your expectations (restroom included)?

_____ How likely will you recommend us to your friends?

Additional comments: _____

Please fill out your information to receive our specials. We will respect your privacy.
Name _____ Email _____
Address _____ Phone _____
City _____ State _____ Zip _____

Supplement 8

- Reverse Side -

YOUR LOGO HERE

Postage will be paid

Business Reply Mail
FIRST_CLASS MAIL PERMIT NO. XXX

Postage will be paid by addressee

Simple Solutions for Selling
Street Address
Address 2
City, ST ZIP Code

www.SimpleSolutionsForSelling.com

YOUR LOGO HERE

Postage will be paid

Business Reply Mail
FIRST_CLASS MAIL PERMIT NO. XXX

Postage will be paid by addressee

Simple Solutions for Selling
Street Address
Address 2
City, ST ZIP Code

www.SimpleSolutionsForSelling.com

YOUR LOGO HERE

Postage will be paid

Business Reply Mail
FIRST_CLASS MAIL PERMIT NO. XXX

Postage will be paid by addressee

Simple Solutions for Selling
Street Address
Address 2
City, ST ZIP Code

www.SimpleSolutionsForSelling.com

YOUR LOGO HERE

Postage will be paid

Business Reply Mail
FIRST_CLASS MAIL PERMIT NO. XXX

Postage will be paid by addressee

Simple Solutions for Selling
Street Address
Address 2
City, ST ZIP Code

www.SimpleSolutionsForSelling.com

Supplement 9

Sales Lead Sheet

Sales Lead Sheet

Salesperson:_____   Date:_____

Contact Information		Company Information	
Contact Name:		Company Name:	
Title:		Address:	
Phone #1:	Phone #2:	City:	State:
Fax:	Email:	Website:	Zip:

Opportunity		Qualification	
Product(s):		Budget:	
$:	% Qualify:	Need / Desire:	
Follow-up:		Timeframe:	

Notes:

Sales Spreadsheet (Archive)

Lead Spreadsheet

Date	Name	Phone #1	Phone #2	Email	Company	Address	City	St.	Zip
1.2.2012	Sample Customer	321.654.9876	321.654.9876	scustomer@usa.com	Acme Inc.	123 Broad St.	Anywhere	ZA	12345

Product(s)	$	% Qualify	Follow-up	Notes
Jewelry	$1,000.00	99%	1.9.2012	Customer is very excited!

Website
www.acme.com

Supplement 11

Applicant Phone Screening Form

APPLICANT PHONE SCREENING FORM

Date ___/___/___

Applicant Name	Product Background	Retail/Sales Background	Availability/ Schedule	Location/Travel Requirements	Salary Desired	Interview Scheduled

Supplement 12

Interview Questions
for New Applicants

- Remember to avoid the following topics: Age, Race, Religion & Lifestyle

1. Tell me about yourself? (family, hobbies etc...)

2. Do you have reliable transportation?

3. What are your views regarding being on time and reliable for work?

4. What do you like about your current job?

5. If you could, what would you change about your current job?

6. What would your current/previous supervisor say about you?

7. Why did you leave your last place of employment?

8. Did you have a sales goal at your previous employer?

9. How often did you meet and exceed your goals?

10. What sets you apart from other employees at your current or previous job?

11. What three words would you use to describe yourself?

12. Are you looking for a job or a career?

13. What do you look for in a career?

14. What long term goals do you have? (3-5 yr. & 5-10 yr.)

15. Why would you like to work here?

Supplement 12
Interview Questions for New Applicants - Page 2

16. What is your perception of the business?

17. Why do you feel that you would be a good salesperson?

18. How do you deal with rejection?

19. How familiar are you with our product?

20. How would you handle an angry customer?

21. Have you had any specific sales training?

22. What would help you to improve your skills?

23. How would you go about creating excellent customer service?

24. Why should we hire you over anyone else?

25. What is your biggest weakness that you want to improve? How?

26. What is your greatest strength that you would bring to our company?

Supplement 13

Interview Analysis Form

Name _____   Date ___ / ___ / _____

Traits	Unsatisfactory	Some Deficiences	Satisfactory	Exceptional	Outstanding	Score
	1	2	3	4	5	
Product Knowledge	No knowledge of products & industry	Slight knowledge of products & industry	Familiar with products & industry	Very familiar with products & industry	Extensive knowledge of products & industry	
Sales / Retail Experience	No experience	Very little experience	2 or more years experience	5 or more years experience	10 or more years experience	
Ability to Communicate	Could not communicate well	Some difficulties- could impact job negatively	Sufficient for job performance	Above average communication skills	Outstanding communication skills	
Ability to Work with Others	Would not work well with others	Some difficulties - may impact job negatively	Sufficient for job performance	Above average- demonstrating leadership qualities	Outstanding - team player & leader	
Interest in Position & Company	Did not show any interest	Slight interest	Appeared interested	Very interested. Like this type of work	Specifically looking for this type of job	
Motivation & Drive	None shown	Shows little desire to succeed	Average drive	Highly motivated	Extremely motivated. Wants to be the best	
Appearance (in relation to job)	Very sloppy, not appropriate for interview	Less than satisfactory, needs improvement	Properly dressed and groomed	Above average grooming	Excellent appearance, very professional	
Personality (in relation to job)	Not acceptable	Some deficiencies	Satisfactory	Outgoing and enthusiastic	Extremely outgoing & enthusiastic	
Overall Demeanor / Confidence	Not acceptable	Some deficiencies	Satisfactory	Above average	Extremely confident	
Employment History	Not acceptable	Has large gaps in employment history	Satisfactory	No gaps in employment history	Was recruited for industry!	
TOTAL SCORE						

Rejection Letter for Applications

Date

Name of Applicant

Applicant's Address

Dear (*Applicant's Name*):

We appreciate your interest in (*Company Name*) and the position of (*Name of Position*) for which you applied. After reviewing the applications received by the deadline, yours was not selected for further consideration.

The selection committee appreciates the time you invested in your application. We encourage you to apply for posted and advertised positions in our company, for which you qualify, in the future.

We wish you every personal and professional success with your job search and in the future. Thank you, again, for your interest in our company.

Regards,

Name and Signature

Rejection Letter for Job Interviews

Date

Name of Applicant

Applicant's Address

Dear (*Applicant's Name*):

As you know, we interviewed a number of candidates for the (*Name of Job*) position, and we have determined that another candidate is the most qualified for the requirements of our opening. So, the purpose of this letter is to let you know that you have not been selected for the position and that we have offered the position to another candidate.

Thank you so much for taking the time to come to (*Company Name*) to meet our interview team. We enjoyed meeting you and our discussions.

Please feel free to apply for open positions, for which you qualify, in our company in the future.

We wish you every personal and professional success with your job search and in the future. Thank you for your interest in our organization.

Best Regards,

Name and Signature

Job Offer Letter

Date
Name
Address

Dear _____:

It is my pleasure to extend the following offer of employment to you on behalf of (*company name*). This offer is contingent upon your passing our mandatory drug screen, our receipt of your college transcripts, and (*any other contingencies you may wish to state*).

Title: _____

Reporting Relationship: The position will report to:
_____

Job Description is attached.

Base Salary: Will be paid in bi-weekly installments of $_____, which is equivalent to $_____ on an annual basis, and subject to deductions for taxes and other withholdings as required by law or the policies of the company.

Non-Compete Agreement: Our standard non-compete agreement must be signed prior to start.

Benefits: The current, standard company health, life, disability and dental insurance coverage are generally supplied per company policy. Eligibility for other benefits, including the 401(k) and tuition reimbursement, will generally take place per company policy. Employee contribution to payment for benefit plans is determined annually.

Vacation and Personal Emergency Time Off: Vacation is accrued at (*xx*) hours per pay period, which is equivalent to two weeks on an annual basis. Personal days are generally accrued per company policy.
Start Date: _____

Supplement 16
Page 2

Car/Phone/Travel Allowance: Normal and reasonable expenses will be reimbursed on a monthly basis per company policy and upon completion of the appropriate expense request form.

Your employment with (Company Name) is at-will and either party can terminate the relationship at any time with or without cause and with or without notice.

You acknowledge that this offer letter, (*along with the final form of any referenced documents*), represents the entire agreement between you and (*Company Name*) and that no verbal or written agreements, promises or representations that are not specifically stated in this offer, are or will be binding upon (*Company Name*).

If you are in agreement with the above outline, please sign below. This offer is in effect for (*generally, five business days*).

Signatures:

_____
(*Company Name*)

_____
Date

_____
(*Candidate's Name*)

_____
Date

Write a Job description

Job title:_____

Reports to:_____

Hours/location: _____

Job duties and responsibilities:

1. _____

2. _____

3. _____

4. _____

5. _____

6. _____

7. _____

8. _____

Work environment and reporting relationship within the company: _____

_____

Required qualifications of candidate (specific skills, education, years of

experience, certifications, etc.): _____

_____

Other necessary skills, including personal characteristics:

_____

Salary/hourly wage, benefits, other compensation:_____

Weekly "To Do" list

Weekly "To Do" List

Date___/___/___

Priority	ITEMS TO BE COMPLETED	Date Completed
A = 24 hours / B = 48 hours / C = by end of work week / D = Ongoing		

Supplement 19
Store Schedule

Store Schedule   Store_____ Month/Year_____

NAME	SUN	MON	TUE	WED	THUR	FRI	SAT	HOURS

NAME	SUN	MON	TUE	WED	THUR	FRI	SAT	HOURS

NAME	SUN	MON	TUE	WED	THUR	FRI	SAT	HOURS

NAME	SUN	MON	TUE	WED	THUR	FRI	SAT	HOURS

NAME	SUN	MON	TUE	WED	THUR	FRI	SAT	HOURS

Store Budget: Full Time_____   Part Time:_____   Total_____

www.SimpleSolutionsForSelling.com   Supplement 19

Daily Store Sales Spreadsheet

Store Sales DAILY Spreadsheet — Store Number: 3663 — Store Name: Sample Company — Month: August — Year: 2011

Date	Forecast (Cumulative)	Percent +/-	Current Year's Direct Sales (Cumulative)	Category 1 Group A Daily Total	Category A Cumulative	Category 2 Group A Daily Total	Category 2 Group B Daily Total	Total Category 2 Daily Total	Total Category 2 Cumulative	Category 3 Daily Total	Category 3 Cumulative	Category 4 Daily Total	Category 4 Cumulative	Total Items Daily	Total Items Cumul.	Leads Daily	Leads Cumul.	Special Units Daily	Special Cumul.
1	1,200.00	18%	1,330.78	230.00	230.00	200.50	50.63	251.13	251.13	60.00	60.00	789.65	789.65	311	311	6	6	2	2
2	2,400.00	22%	2,926.58	300.00	530.00	250.13	75.00	325.13	576.26	120.00	180.00	850.67	1,640.32	336	647	6	12	1	3
3	3,600.00	18%	4,242.30	420.00	950.00	120.85	56.00	176.65	752.91	120.00	240.00	659.57	2,299.89	319	966	6	18	1	4
4	4,800.00	19%	5,698.76	400.00	1,350.00	54.32	45.00	99.32	852.23	60.00	300.00	896.64	3,196.53	300	1,266	5	23	3	7
5	6,000.00	16%	6,963.36	300.00	1,650.00	26.35	35.00	61.35	913.58	120.00	420.00	783.25	3,979.78	298	1,564	7	30	2	9
6	7,200.00	14%	8,236.58	230.00	1,880.00	12.85	95.00	107.85	1,021.43	240.00	660.00	695.37	4,675.15	302	1,866	5	35	2	11
7	8,400.00	16%	9,730.48	100.00	1,980.00	85.64	85.00	170.64	1,192.07	240.00	900.00	983.26	5,658.41	285	2,151	6	41	1	12
8	9,600.00	10%	10,543.49	130.00	2,110.00	98.34	65.00	163.34	1,355.41	120.00	1,020.00	399.67	6,058.08	275	2,426	8	49	2	14
9	10,800.00	8%	11,616.25	150.00	2,260.00	54.12	32.00	86.12	1,441.53	180.00	1,200.00	659.64	6,717.72	267	2,693	5	54	3	17
10	12,000.00	7%	12,852.16	200.00	2,460.00	23.32	65.00	88.32	1,529.85	180.00	1,380.00	765.59	7,483.31	285	2,978	6	60	2	19
11	13,200.00	5%	13,859.78	130.00	2,590.00	45.97	65.00	90.97	1,620.82	120.00	1,500.00	665.65	8,148.96	280	3,258	6	66	2	21
12	14,400.00	3%	14,959.73	110.00	2,700.00	65.41	25.00	90.41	1,711.23	60.00	1,560.00	733.54	8,888.50	275	3,533	8	74	1	22
13	15,600.00	2%	15,987.29	90.00	2,790.00	27.98	85.00	112.98	1,824.21	60.00	1,620.00	764.68	9,653.18	298	3,831	7	81	0	22
14	16,800.00	0%	16,824.77	80.00	2,870.00	32.85	75.00	107.85	1,932.06	120.00	1,740.00	629.53	10,282.71	267	4,098	4	85	2	24
15	18,000.00	-3%	17,493.77	60.00	2,930.00	34.42	45.00	79.42	2,011.48	60.00	1,800.00	469.58	10,752.29	245	4,343	7	92	2	26
16	19,200.00	-4%	18,338.72	90.00	3,020.00	65.98	32.00	97.98	2,109.46	120.00	1,920.00	536.97	11,289.26	258	4,601	8	100	1	27
17	20,400.00	-4%	19,637.85	70.00	3,090.00	147.86	65.00	212.86	2,322.32	180.00	2,100.00	838.27	12,125.53	268	4,869	9	109	4	31
18	21,600.00	-3%	21,054.77	150.00	3,240.00	195.64	65.00	260.64	2,572.96	180.00	2,280.00	836.28	12,961.81	285	5,154	6	115	3	34
19	22,800.00	-2%	22,301.29	120.00	3,360.00	230.98	32.00	262.98	2,835.94	240.00	2,520.00	623.54	13,585.35	275	5,429	5	120	3	37
20	24,000.00	-3%	22,357.31	90.00	3,450.00	245.35	45.00	290.35	3,126.29	180.00	2,700.00	495.67	14,081.02	285	5,714	5	125	2	39
21	25,200.00	-3%	24,428.11	80.00	3,530.00	180.85	16.00	196.85	3,323.14	120.00	2,820.00	674.95	14,755.97	291	6,005	7	132	1	40
22	26,400.00	-3%	25,735.62	250.00	3,780.00	256.24	16.00	272.24	3,594.38	120.00	2,940.00	685.17	15,421.14	245	6,250	5	137	2	42
23	27,600.00	-2%	26,950.94	180.00	3,960.00	180.56	95.00	275.56	3,869.94	240.00	3,180.00	559.86	15,981.00	237	6,487	3	140	2	44
24	28,800.00	-2%	28,224.50	160.00	4,120.00	150.67	85.00	235.67	4,105.61	240.00	3,420.00	597.97	16,578.97	249	6,736	5	145	2	46
25	30,000.00	-2%	29,451.76	160.00	4,280.00	267.51	35.00	302.51	4,408.12	300.00	3,720.00	464.67	17,043.64	261	6,997	2	147	3	49
26	31,200.00	-1%	31,017.74	170.00	4,450.00	195.74	64.00	259.74	4,667.86	180.00	3,900.00	956.24	17,999.88	237	7,234	5	152	2	51
27	32,400.00	0%	32,263.61	120.00	4,570.00	202.45	43.00	245.45	5,093.31	120.00	4,020.00	654.32	18,654.20	312	7,546	4	156	2	53
28	33,600.00	1%	33,786.53	130.00	4,700.00	269.46	65.00	334.46	5,353.77	60.00	4,080.00	998.56	19,652.76	310	7,856	4	160	0	54
29	34,800.00	2%	35,461.36	150.00	4,850.00	341.95	86.00	427.95	5,781.72	240.00	4,140.00	1,056.88	20,709.64	259	8,155	6	166	3	57
30	36,000.00	2%	36,742.61	120.00	4,970.00	240.40	95.00	335.40	6,117.12	240.00	4,380.00	565.85	21,275.49	283	8,438	4	170	2	59
31	#DIV/0!				4,970.00			0.00	6,117.12		4,380.00		21,275.49		8,438		170		59

MONTHLY TOTALS	36,742.61	
MONTHLY FORECAST	36,000.00	
Last Year:	34,552.95	
% to LY:	106	
% to Forecast:	102%	

Supplement 21

Weekly Store Evaluation Form

Store Name_____ Date_____

____ Store windows are clean and signage is accurate

____ Carpets clean and vacuumed, tile floors clean (sweep and mop)

____ Cash stands neat and free of clutter - No Junk, No Toys!

____ Lead sheets-1-2 leads per shift per employee

____ Special orders caught up within 48 hours

____ Review the Weekly Store Report (WSR) with store staff. Discuss five
areas of improvement (List in notes section)

____ Product racks organized, no overstock on sales floor

____ Merchandise on walls neat & organized by sections

____ Current promotional pricing complete and accurate, fliers displayed

____ Price labels are complete with correct price - audit 10 items

____ Answering the phone (phone skills) hungry, high energy, extracting
leads, asking questions?

____ Waiting on customers. On sales floor, probing, engaging in
conversation, suggestive selling?

____ Stockroom is clean and organized

____ Break area is clean and organized

____ On Hold items - customers called within 30 days

____ Layaway payments are current on all.

____ Scheduled employee hours are meeting or under budget

____ Payroll recap - at budget

____ Goal board is up to date, motivational and accurate

____ Store email account has appropriate content and usage

Supplement 21
Page 2

Notes _____

_____

_____

_____

_____

_____

_____

_____

_____

_____

Weekly Sales Report_____

_____

_____

_____

_____

_____

_____

_____

_____

Overall Assessment of Store _____

_____

_____

_____

_____

_____

_____

_____

Supplement 22

Quarterly Store Evaluation Form

Store Evaluation Form

Store Name: Date:

Manager:

Neatness & Store Appearance:

1. Front & Back Counter Area / Cash Stands (6 points max)

Counters clear of any papers/misc. product	
Glass wiped with cleaning product	
Office supplies are neat & organized	
Organizer bins are in order and labeled	
Reference binders & staff binders are neat and labeled	
Impulse items are merchandised	
Comments:	Total:
	0

2. General Floor Displays (9 points max)

Product racks are full and merchandised to company standards	
Merchandise is clean and dust free	
All display cases are clean and well organized	
Out of stock (empty pegs) kept to a minimum	
Merchandise is off the floor	
Pricing on merchandise is accurate and neatly placed on product	
Price tags are placed on product in a uniform fashion	
Product is positioned at the front tip of the merchandising pegs	
Product is positioned at the front edge of the shelves and in straight lines	
Comments:	Total:
	0

3. Wall Displays of product (9 points max)

Full assortment represented and ready to sell	
Merchandise is clean and dust free	
Merchandising as per company standards	
Merchandise organized by sections with separation	
Out of stock (empty pegs) kept to a minimum	
Pricing on merchandise is accurate and neatly placed on product	
Price tags are placed on product in a uniform fashion	
Product is positioned at the front tip of the merchandising pegs	
Product is positioned at the front edge of the shelves and in straight lines	
Comments:	Total:
	0

Supplement 22
Quarterly Store Evaluation Form – Page 2

Store Evaluation Form

4. In-store Signage (6 points max)

Store hours sign is correct and posted at the front entrance	
General merchandise pricing labels at 100%lebels at 100%	
Special product is promoted properly	
Window posters are presented properly	
General merchandise pricing labels at 100%lebels at 100%	
Special promotional signage presented properly	
Comments:	Total:
	0

5. Floor and Fixture Cleanliness (7 points max)

Carpets vacuumed	
Tile floors look clean and polished	
Trash cans emptied nightly	
In store fixtures clean and well maintained	
Ceiling tiles free of stains, vents clean	
Ceiling vents are clean	
Store has fresh and clean presence and smell	
Comments:	Total:
	0

6. Stockroom (8 points max)

Break area clean and organized	
Special orders and on hold area clearly marked and product seperated	
Incoming bin/shelf clearly marked	
Outgoing bin/shelf clearly marked	
Stock shelves clearly marked with appropriate product	
All paperwork organized and in correct place	
Extra supplies in corect place and organized	
Utility items (broom, mop, vacuum, etc..) in correct place	
Comments:	Total:
	0

7. Restroom (4 points max)

Appropriate paper products/soap & supplies in storage cabinet	
Glass/sink/toilet are clean	
Floor clean, free from product	
Ceiling vent is clean & operational	
Comments:	Total:
	0

Supplement 22
Quarterly Store Evaluation Form - Page 3

Store Evaluation Form

8. Lighting (4 points max)

All light bulbs operating	
All ballast operating	
Front signage working properly on a timer	
Outdoor lighting functioning properly	
Comments:	Total:
	0

Total (Out of 53)	0

Organization:

1. Sales and Sales Culture (6 points max)

Communication board displayed in back roon	
Memo notices / store updates signed by every employee	
Dress code standards posted and followed by all	
Company philosophy of sales posted & being followed by employees	
Sales contest or company sales challenge being promoted	
Sales staff knows the current company promotions	
Comments:	Total:
	0

2. Networking / Lead Sheets (4 points max)

Every sales person has his/her own lead sheet	
Every sales person has at least one lead per **4** hour shift written	
Appointments and follow up written clearly in sales binder	
Lead sheets clear of business cards/extra pieces of paper	
Comments:	Total:
	0

3. Tasks / Goals (4 points max)

Employee goals posted on communication board	
"Personell Duties" list posted and up to date	
Store "Daily To-Do List" posted and up to date	
"Weekly Store Report" posted and most current	
Comments:	Total:
	0

4. Product - Special Orders / On Holds (4 points max)

Special order file folder organized by last name	
Special order deposit taken for all accessories & product ordered	
Packing slips and receivers well managed to company policy	
All on-hold product over two weeks old called and/or put back	
Comments:	Total:
	0

Supplement 22
Quarterly Store Evaluation Form - Page 4

Store Evaluation Form

5. Schedule (5 points max)

Posted on communication board	
Hours are on target or under budget	
All sales and store meetings are scheduled and employee hours are adjusted	
Overtime policy is posted and being followed	
Hours maximized for best performance	
Comments:	Total:
	0

6. Management / Misc. Items (4 points max)

Customer relations are being managed, no outstanding issues	
Nightly business reconciled properly and up to date	
Appropriate music playing in store	
Employee parking regulations followed	
Comments:	Total:
	0

Total (Out of 27) `0`

Grand Total (Out of 80) `0`

Scale:

75 - 80 Superior

70 - 74 Excellent

65 - 69 Good

60 - 64 Needs Improvement

59 or Less - Unacceptable, Needs Immediate Improvement

Additional Comments:

Supplement 23
Yearly Marketing Calendar 2012

January

Month		1250 units			
	2	9	16	23	30
Sales Goal / Week of (Mon. Start)	New Years		Industry Conference	Martin Luther King Day	
Key Dates & Events					Sales Promo (Offer)
Sales Promotions		Product Brochures	Industry Pres.		
Presentations			Industry Conference		
Public Relations		Pre Conf		Post Conf.	
Press Releases		Keyword/Search Advertising			
Online	Promote Conference				
Keyword/Search		Online Auction & Stores			
Site Targeted Ads		Online Directory Listings & Classified			
Online Stores		Affiliate Recruitment Incentive Program			
Online Directory Listings & Classified	Facebook Announce	Pre Conf Tweets	Live Tweets	Post Conf. Tweets	XYZ Tweets
Affiliate Programs	Visit us at conference and receive free gift		Recap, Live Blog	Upcoming Sls Promo	
Social Media - Twitter, Facebook, YouTube...	Visit us at conference and receive free gift			Upcoming Sls Promo	
Blog/RSS	Visit us at conference and receive free gift			Upcoming Sls Promo	Online coupon
Email				Conf Highlights	
Website Messaging			XYZ Campaign QR Code - product info		
Mobile			XYZ Campaign		
Advertising			XYZ Campaign		
TV			XYZ Campaign with QR Code		
Radio	Teaser for XYZ Campaign				
Print					
Outdoor		Email Customer Satisfaction Survey			
Research		Brand Metrics, Web Analytics, ROI			
Customer Surveys					
Marketing Effectiveness					

Sales & Management Training Modules: Solutions For Selling

Available at www.SolutionsForSelling.com

The "**Sales & Management Training Modules: Solutions For Selling**" publication contains each chapter of this book formatted as a training session for your sales staff and management team. Each module also includes discussion questions to facilitate a meaningful interaction. All modules are also included on a disk allowing you to edit and adapt these presentations for your specific needs.

Also included on the disc are the supplemental documents and forms that are discussed in this publication. These documents will help simplify the daily operations of your business and aid with the concepts being taught in this book. All documents, forms and spreadsheets are fully editable and adaptable for your business. A sample of each can be viewed in the "Supplements" section of this book. (page 157)

This publication is available at **www.SolutionsForSelling.com** and the contents can be viewed on the next page.

Contents for *"Sales & Management Training Modules: Solutions For Selling"*

Sales Training Modules

Management Training Modules

Supplemental Documents and Forms

Bibliography

Carnegie, Dale *"How to Win Friends & Influence People"* – Pocket Books / Simon & Schuster, Inc. 1998

Covey, Stephen *"The 7 habits of Highly Effective People: Power Lessons in Personal Change"* – Free Press, Simon & Schuster, Inc. 2004

Friedman, Harry *"No Thanks, I'm Just Looking! Retail Sales Techniques for Turning Shoppers into Buyers"* – John Wiley & Sons 1992

Gladwell, Malcolm *"The Tipping Point: How Little Things Can Make a Big Difference"* – Little Brown and Company 2000

Gladwell, Malcolm *"The Tipping Point: How Little Things Can Make a Big Difference"* – Little Brown and Company *2008*

Hopkins, Tom *"How to Master the Art of Selling"* – Writers of the Round Table Press 2005

Jantsch, John *"Duct Tape Marketing: The World's Most Practical Small Business Marketing Guide"* – Thomas Nelson Inc. 2011

Maxwell, John C. *"Attitude 101"*, *"Developing the leader Within You"* – Thomas Nelson Inc. 2003

Ziglar, Zig *"Selling 101: What Every Successful Sales Professional Needs to Know" 2003*

Ziglar, Zig *"Secrets of Closing the Sale"* Baker Publishing Group 2003

www.SolutionsForSelling.com

www.ingramcontent.com/pod-product-compliance
Lightning Source LLC
Chambersburg PA
CBHW060527210326
41519CB00014B/3146